STARS
OF THE MAJOR LEAGUES

Here are the action-packed stories of
some of baseball's brightest young stars.
Dave Klein traces the ups and downs in
the exciting careers of Johnny Bench,
Cesar Cedeno, Catfish Hunter, Bobby Murcer,
Nate Colbert, John Mayberry, Carlton Fisk,
Bobby Bonds and Ferguson Jenkins.

Illustrated with photographs

STARS
OF THE MAJOR LEAGUES

BY DAVE KLEIN

MAJOR LEAGUE
LIBRARY

Random House · New York

PHOTOGRAPH CREDITS: Clifton Boutelle: 27, 40, 87, 90, 103, 117, 139; Malcolm Emmons: 10, 72, 100; United Press International: endpapers, 2-3, 13, 15, 20, 24, 36, 38, 51, 53, 57, 60, 67, 69, 75, 81, 92, 97, 109, 124, 130, 133, 145; Wide World Photos: 33, 47, 50, 112-113, 119, 126-127.
Cover photograph by Clifton Boutelle.

Library of Congress Cataloging in Publication Data
Klein, Dave. Stars of the major leagues. (Major league library)
SUMMARY: Profiles of nine major league baseball stars: Johnny Bench, Cesar Cedeno, Jim "Catfish" Hunter, Bobby Murcer, Nate Colbert, John Mayberry, Carlton Fisk, Bobby Bonds, and Ferguson Jenkins.
1. Baseball—Biography—Juvenile literature. [1. Baseball—Biography] I. Title.
GV865.A1K57 1974   796.357′092′2 [B][920] 73-18739
ISBN 0-394-82762-7   ISBN 0-394-92762-1 (lib. bdg.)

To **Aaron and Mindy,** *Already Hall of Famers*

CONTENTS

INTRODUCTION

Every few years a new batch of fans discover the fun and excitement of professional baseball. And every few years a new batch of major league stars is ready to perform for them.

Most major league hopefuls never make it any farther than a minor league team, such as Pawtucket, Rhode Island, or Greenville, North Carolina. But the most talented—and the luckiest—finally arrive in the big leagues, hoping to make a mark with the power of their swing, the speed of their fast ball or the grace of their fielding. Of course many of those new arrivals soon find themselves back in the minors— but a few *do* make a permanent mark on baseball.

Stars of the Major Leagues is designed to introduce those new heroes to some new fans. As with most such books, there could be a far longer list compiled. But the nine players represented here have much to tell about the boyhood experiences that brought them to the majors—and the hard work and rewards they found along the way.

A generation ago this book would have included players like Willie Mays and Mickey Mantle, Henry Aaron, Roberto Clemente and Sandy Koufax. They became superstars, and even legends, in their own day.

But today's stars are tomorrow's Hall of Famers. For who will challenge the records of Mantle and the rest? Perhaps a Johnny Bench or a Cesar Cedeno or one of the others in this book.

This question won't be answered for years to come. But one thing is sure: as soon as these young stars have set their records, a new wave of major leaguers will be ready to challenge them.

After all, that's what baseball is all about. So, of course, is this book.

JOHNNY BENCH

After just five years as a major league catcher for the Cincinnati Reds, Johnny Bench had already racked up an incredible list of achievements:

- He had been named Rookie of the Year, at the age of 20.
- He had been named the National League's Most Valuable Player twice.
- He had played in five All-Star games.
- He had participated in two World Series.
- He had led the league in home runs twice and in runs batted in twice.
- And he had won the Golden Glove award for catchers in each of the five years.

Not bad . . . not bad at all for a kid from Binger,

Oklahoma—"a town so small," according to Bench, "that folks driving down the highway missed it if they sneezed . . . and if someone asked how to get to Binger, we'd tell them 'oh, it's about two miles beyond the resume speed sign.' "

Johnny Bench was truly a superstar. In fact, many people considered him the finest catcher in the history of the majors—and that included all the great Hall of Fame catchers like Bill Dickey, Roy Campanella, Gabby Hartnett, Mickey Cochrane and Yogi Berra.

Bench could do everything a catcher had to do, and he did it better than anyone else.

He hit with dynamite power. He fielded bunts and grounders with grace and quickness. He handled pitchers with the skill and intelligence of a much older man. And he could make that long throw from behind home plate to second to cut down a would-be base-stealer with shocking ease.

Was there nothing Johnny Bench couldn't do well? "Yes," he often admitted, "lose. I am a terrible loser, maybe the world's worst. I sulk and I get mean and irritable. I just hate it."

Fortunately, the way he played, neither Johnny nor his Reds had to worry much about losing.

Johnny Lee Bench, a part-Choctaw Indian, was born on December 7, 1947, in Oklahoma City, Oklahoma, a short way from Binger. Almost from the time he could walk, Johnny wanted to be a

Cincinnati's Johnny Bench, as effective at the plate as behind it, swings for the fences in a 1973 game against the New York Mets.

baseball player. His father, Ted, had a lot to do with that. Mr. Bench was a semi-pro catcher, and he wanted his son to be the major leaguer he wasn't lucky enough to be.

Johnny had two older brothers, Ted, Jr., and William, and all three Bench boys received the expert teachings of their father. But when Ted, Sr., realized that Johnny had the most natural talent, he concentrated his teaching on his youngest boy.

"My dad taught me to play," Johnny recalled, "and I know I would never have made it without his help. He had me throwing and catching when I was five years old. But you know, I really had to work at it. I missed a lot of boyhood fun because I was so serious about becoming a major leaguer.

"He never really pushed me to be a player, because I wanted to be one anyway," Bench continued. "What he did was make sure I could play whenever I wanted to. He organized a Little League team right in Binger so I could play. But we just didn't have a lot of boys in town—not nearly enough for a whole league—so he used to drive me to Fort Cobb [about 20 miles away] for me to play in their league. It was a bigger town."

Johnny played baseball all through school, getting better and better each year. There is no doubt that Ted Bench's constant instruction was what turned Johnny from "just another good schoolboy catcher" into one of the best catchers in major league history.

Bench blocks the plate and tags Chicago's Randy Hundley out at home. Hundley tried to score on a squeeze play.

"We used to practice all the minor things, the details that kids don't usually worry about," Johnny remembered. "Like the throw to second. Okay, most kids with a strong arm can throw from home plate to second. But my dad wanted me to throw hard, quick and low. So he made me practice throwing to center field. I guess it was two hundred, two hundred fifty feet away. When I could do that well, second base was no problem at all."

Indeed, one Cincinnati second baseman later marveled that "Johnny's peg to second never gets more than two feet off the ground, but no lower, either. It hits your glove with a pop, and it's right where it should be to get a runner. I know some pitchers who wish they threw as hard as he does."

Ted Bench knew another thing about catching. In schoolboy games nobody really wants to be the catcher. There are too many foul tips that sting the fingers, too many hard fouls that spin off the bat and into the face, too many low pitches that bend the fingers backwards.

"There is always a need for catchers," he told his son. "It's not a glamour position."

So Johnny kept catching. But he also found time to pitch. When he was 15, he spent a summer playing American Legion baseball and, when he wasn't behind the plate, he built a 16–1 record as a pitcher.

Basketball was another Bench sport. When he was

a senior at Binger High, Johnny averaged nearly 30 points a game, made a high school All-America team and could have played college basketball as a 6-foot, 190-pound guard.

In the spring of 1965, Johnny's senior year, the baseball scouts all knew about this Oklahoma super-kid. They came in groups to see him play, and they began making attractive offers. (There was no draft of players, so any team could make him an offer.) But Johnny was also receiving college scholarship offers. Not only was he a great athlete, he had been valedictorian of his high school class.

Through the spring Bench tried to decide between baseball and college. He finally chose baseball. "I passed up the chance to go to college because I wanted to be a major league player right away," Johnny explained. "I might do it differently now."

His baseball idol was fellow Oklahoman Mickey Mantle, and for a while Johnny thought he would like to play for Mantle's Yankees. However, when Cincinnati offered him a $10,000 bonus, he forgot the Yanks and signed with the Reds.

But Bench almost didn't make it to the majors—or even the minors.

That spring, shortly before he signed with Cincinnati, Johnny almost lost his life. His Binger High team was returning from a game in nearby Anadarko when the school bus lost its brakes, crashed into a guard rail, flipped over and rolled down an embankment.

Two of Johnny's teammates were thrown out of the bus and killed, and when the bus finally stopped rolling, Johnny was found half-in, half-out.

"It sure was a rotten way to start a career," he once reflected. "Two of my friends were killed."

But Bench was off to Tampa, Florida, home of the Reds' Class A team in the Florida State League.

It took a while for the 17-year-old catcher to successfully compete against much older men. But even that first summer, no one doubted Johnny's potential. He hit .248, with a pair of home runs, 35 RBI's and 53 hits in 68 games.

The next year Bench moved up to the Peninsula team of the Carolinas League, and his statistics improved in the atmosphere of better competition. He hit .294, drove in 68 runs, hammered out 22 homers and collected 103 hits in 98 games.

Johnny Bench was really on his way. It seemed nothing could stop him now.

Next stop: Buffalo of the International League. But Bench played in only one game in 1966, after being involved in an automobile accident which sidelined him for just about the entire season.

The next year Johnny came roaring back. He tore up the International League pitching with 23 homers, 68 RBI's and a .259 batting average. He also led the league in assists. Not surprisingly, he was named

Minor League Player of the Year for 1967.

At the end of the Buffalo season Johnny was called up to Cincinnati and finished the major league schedule as a member of the Reds. In 26 games he got to bat 86 times—long enough to hit his first major league homer and drive in six runs, but not long enough to jeopardize his rookie status for 1968.

And that was a good thing, for Johnny Bench had big plans for the year of 1968.

"I knew when the season ended in '67 that I had a pretty good chance to win the regular job," he said. "I wanted to do that very badly."

In 1967 the Reds' catchers had been Johnny Edwards and Don Pavletich, both good but ordinary performers. In 1968 the catcher was Johnny Bench.

"He just took over, a twenty-year-old kid," said Jim Maloney, one of the league's best pitchers for many years. "I remember one game, I had two strikes on a hitter and he had gone for fastballs both times. I wanted to get him with a third, but Bench signaled for a curve. I shook him off and he did it again, and I shook him off and he finally came out to the mound and yelled at me.

"You know? I threw the curve and we got the batter by a foot. He was right. Imagine, a twenty-year-old kid."

The other players and managers in the league quickly saw that Johnny was indeed one of those rare special stars. "I've never seen a man that good

Bench grimaces as Cardinal Lou Brock slams into him in a 1968 game, but he tags Brock for the out. Bench was Rookie of the Year in 1968.

at his age," said Dodger manager Walter Alston. "I guess he'll be the All-Star catcher for ten or twenty years now."

The young rookie started living up to Alston's prediction that very year by being named to his first All-Star team.

By the end of the season, Bench had caught 154 games—a major league record for rookie catchers—and walked off with 15 home runs, 40 doubles, 82 RBI's, a .275 average— and the Rookie of the Year Award tucked in his back pocket. It was the first time a catcher had ever been given that award. Johnny also led the league in putouts, assists and fielding to win the Golden Glove award for catchers.

It was clear that Bench was a very special catcher. After that first major league season no one less than Hall of Famer Ted Williams gave the super-rookie an autographed baseball inscribed: "To Johnny Bench, a Hall of Famer for sure."

It's hard to believe, but in 1969, Bench did even better. He hit more homers (26), drove in more runs (90), collected more hits (156) and had a higher batting average (.293).

Again he was the starting catcher for the National League All-Stars. He went two-for-three, hit a homer, scored twice and drove in two runs.

In 1970, almost impossibly, Bench was better than ever. That was the year he went into orbit as a genuine superstar.

Again he batted .293, but this time he had 177 hits and led the majors with 45 homers and 148 runs batted in. Along with such sluggers as Tony Perez, Pete Rose, Bobby Tolan and Lee May, he led the Reds to the 1970 National League pennant. Cincinnati fans called their team The Big Red Machine—and all agreed that Johnny Bench was the biggest Red of them all.

The Reds swept the Pirates in three games in the National League playoffs. But then they bowed to the Baltimore Orioles in five World Series games. "Just wait till next year," cried the disappointed Cincinnati fans.

But in 1971 the Reds failed to defend even their Western Division crown, falling to fourth place with 79 wins against 83 losses. One of the major reasons for that dismal record was an off season by Johnny Bench.

"I was terrible," he admitted. "It felt to me like the club was down because I was down. We weren't scoring runs, and everything seems to go wrong in those kind of games. After winning so easily in 1970, it was very frustrating."

After the 1971 season Bench went to the Reds' instructional league team in Florida for the winter—not to play, but to think. He decided to drop some of his off-season business interests, lost some weight and studied films of himself and other great hitters.

"It was up to me to prove that 1971 was the mistake, not 1970," he stated. "I really made up my mind to be tougher and more dedicated."

In 1972, Johnny proved the power of positive thinking. In 1971 he had hit .238—in '72 he hit .270. He jumped from 61 RBI's to 125, leading the major leagues in that department. He jumped from 27 homers to 40, again leading both leagues. He also increased his hits from 134 to 145. And to top it all off, he had a stretch of seven homers in five games, which tied a record set in 1929.

Johnny Bench took the Reds on a miracle comeback that saw them climb to the top of their division. With Bench his old self again, the Reds won the 1972 pennant, beating the powerful Pirates in the playoffs.

But Cincinnati lost the World Series again, this time in a seven-game contest against the Oakland A's. Nevertheless, Johnny was the unanimous MVP choice after the Series ended—and the Reds were quite willing to sign him to his first $100,000-plus contract.

"If I had to name the best young hitters in the National League," said Hank Aaron after that season, "I'd have to start with Johnny Bench. He is the best hitter to come along in a long, long time."

Johnny Bench was on top of the world. He had a three-floor condominium apartment in Cincinnati,

The Reds have just lost the seventh game of the 1972 World Series to Oakland, and Bench sits dejectedly in the locker room.

various business deals, endorsements and speaking engagements—more important, he had millions of fans all over the country.

But in November 1972 came a shocking news story. A physical examination of Johnny Bench had shown a spot on his right lung.

No one knew for sure what that meant. It could have been very serious. It could have been cancer. Even after a long series of tests in Cincinnati, Bench's doctor decided that only an exploratory operation would reveal Johnny's true condition.

The surgery was scheduled for the middle of December, so that Johnny would be up in time to celebrate Christmas. He hoped he would have reason to celebrate.

And celebrate he did. The test results were all he could have hoped for. The spot turned out to be a lesion caused by a viral infection. When it was removed, Johnny Bench was in perfect condition again.

"It was such a tremendous relief," he said after the operation. "But in a way, it gave me time to think seriously. I saw that it's important to accomplish goals as soon as possible, and I learned to be very, very thankful for having been given the talents to play baseball. The money . . . the appearances . . . they're secondary. I love this game, and now I can continue to play it. That's what turned out to be the most important thing of all."

CESAR CEDENO

"At twenty-two years of age, Cesar Cedeno is as good or better than Willie Mays was at the same age," Leo Durocher declared. "I don't know whether he can keep this up for twenty years, and I'm not saying he will be better than Mays. But I will say this kid has a chance to be as good. And that's saying a lot."

Coming from Durocher that certainly was saying a lot. For Durocher is probably the one man truly qualified to compare anyone to Mays. Leo managed the New York Giants from 1951, when Mays came up to the major leagues, through 1955. By that time Willie had already established himself as one of baseball's all-time greats.

But for 20 years Durocher refused to compare anyone to Mays. Never did he say "This kid is as good as Willie was" or "I think this one might be a Mays-type player."

Then in 1973, 22 years after he first met Mays, Leo broke his silence of more than two decades.

At that time the 66-year-old Durocher was manager of the Houston Astros. He was managing a young star who deserved comparison with Willie. His name was Cesar Cedeno.

Was he as good as Willie Mays? Could he ever be? Was it possible he could be even better? No one really knew the answers to those questions—certainly not Cedeno.

"I read in the paper I'm the greatest," he said. "I don't know. I try to work hard, always to give one hundred per cent . . . I need to be more consistent . . . sometimes I don't feel like the greatest anything."

Still the comparisons continued—and with good reason.

In Willie Mays' third year as a major leaguer his statistics included a .345 batting average, 41 home runs, 110 RBI's and such extras as 13 triples, 33 doubles and 195 hits.

In Cesar Cedeno's third year he had a .320 batting average, 22 home runs, 82 RBI's, 8 triples, 39 doubles and 179 hits.

Cedeno had other talents that weren't so easy to

Cesar Cedeno relaxes with his biggest fan, manager Leo Durocher.

measure. For example, he was one of the fastest men in the majors—and one of the smartest base runners. Given half a chance, he could stretch singles to doubles and doubles to triples.

He was powerfully built, standing 6-foot-2 and weighing 190 pounds. So Cesar was just as likely to go for distance as to try beating out a grounder.

In center field, he combined his speed with a natural ability to "hear" the crack of the ball against the bat and know where to go for the play. "He's probably the most natural outfielder I've seen since Mays," said Durocher. "You probably won't see a better arm, for instance, in all of baseball."

But even more important, Cedeno had an indescribable talent for "turning on" a crowd that stamped him as special in the field or at bat.

Cesar Cedeno was born in Santo Domingo in 1951—the same year Willie Mays joined the Giants. He was the oldest of five children born to Diogene and Juanita Cedeno.

"We were among the rich people of the island," he laughed, "because we had a car and a television set." Nevertheless, Cesar remembered the day his mother bought him baseball shoes and a glove without telling his father because she knew they really couldn't afford them.

Santo Domingo, the capital city of the island of the Dominican Republic, is roughly 150 miles west of Puerto Rico and 500 miles southeast of the United States. There, just as in the United States, baseball is considered the "national pastime." In fact, the small island has been a real goldmine for major league baseball scouts from the United States. Juan Marichal, Rico Carty and the three Alou brothers—Felipe, Matty and Jesus—were all Dominicans.

"We played baseball all the time, every day," said Cesar, remembering his boyhood. "My father had been a player, too, and I wanted to become the best from my country. My father helped me a lot, because he wanted that, too."

Day after day, Cesar played under the hot Caribbean sun, and soon he began to attract the major league scouts. The New York Mets, St. Louis Cardinals and Houston Astros were all interested in Cedeno.

Houston scouting director Pat Gillick arranged a tryout for Cesar. But Gillick had already seen Cedeno play, and he knew Houston would want to sign him. Gillick had to hurry, because other teams were making offers.

"We had to fool the Cardinals," Gillick remembered. "They had made a low offer and then started raising it by little bits, like from $500 to $750, and then to $1,000. We found out their scout was going to be back the next day with a bigger offer, so we met with Cesar and his parents, and our offer got up to $1,500. Then, to make sure, we said we'd double it if he signed that night. He did. After the tryout we held for him we knew we had a very special baseball player, maybe the best natural talent since Aaron or Mays."

For the relatively small sum of $3,000, the Astros had gotten quite a bargain. Still, it was a lot of money to the boy from Santo Domingo, who at the age of 16, had suddenly become a professional. Cesar Cedeno had a lot to learn.

"He was a young boy, not familiar with the language and very scared," recalled Tony Pacheco, the man who managed Cesar in his first minor league seasons. "I remember his first time at bat he struck out. It was just a spring training game in Florida at the Astros' camp, but he got all upset. He ran off and cried. I found him and, to cheer him up, I told him the next time up he should rip a home run. So he did."

After spring training Cedeno was sent to Covington (Kentucky) in the Appalachian League. There the young rookie built up a .374 average with 49 hits in 36 games. On the strength of that performance, the Astros moved him up to Cocoa in the Carolinas League for the second half of the 1968 season. In his next 69 games, Cesar hit .256 with 46 hits.

Cedeno spent all of 1969 at Peninsula in the Carolinas League. By the end of the season he had collected 5 home runs, 39 RBI's and a league-leading 32 doubles. He hit .274 with 136 hits in 142 games.

More familiar with his new country and more confident as a baseball player, Cesar Cedeno was looking like a sure bet for the majors. So in 1970, Cedeno was sent to Oklahoma City of the American Association, a Triple-A league.

"He was ready for better competition," said Pacheco. "He didn't need to feel his way around any more."

That year was Cesar's best yet. After 54 games he was hitting .373 with 61 RBI's, 14 homers and 87 hits, when the Astros called him up to Houston.

Cedeno's major league career got off to a slow

In one of his early major league games Cedeno dives safely into second base. He was soon a leading base-runner for the Astros.

start. After a few weeks, his batting average was a dismal .204, and he began to lose his confidence. Jimmy Wynn, the Astros' rightfielder, commented: "I think they made a mistake in bringing this kid up. He needed at least another year in the minor leagues."

Wynn, who had lost his center-field position as well as his leadoff batting spot to Cedeno, may have been judging the young rookie harshly. Nevertheless, it was true that Cedeno had looked a lot better in the minors than he did in Houston.

But then on July 11, less than a month after he had joined the Astros, Cesar got a chance to prove his critics wrong. Houston was playing San Francisco—Willie Mays and the Giants—in the Astrodome. The teams were locked up in a tie.

As the game dragged on, Cesar was booed by the hometown crowd. He had struck out early in the game. Then he struck out in the ninth inning with a runner on third. He struck out again in the twelfth inning, this time with the bases loaded.

In the 14th inning, still hitless, he came up to bat for the eighth time. The boos thundered down.

And then Cesar singled.

The next man up got a hit, too. It was a short single, and the rightfielder got to it quickly—but not quickly enough. Using the element of surprise, Cesar rounded second and never once hesitated. He made it to third easily, ahead of the hurried, desperate throw.

The next man up hit a short sacrifice fly ball. Cesar tagged up and scored, beating the throw home. The game was over, at last—thanks to Cesar Cedeno.

The Astros had won the game, and Cesar had regained his confidence. "I was nervous in the major leagues," he later recalled. "I was trying too hard, like that first time I went to bat in spring training. When the fans started to boo me I just tried harder and that doesn't do any good. But then I saw that I could do the same things in Houston that I did in Oklahoma City, and it got better."

For the rest of the season Cedeno went on hitting streaks—hitting safely in seven straight games, then seven more, then nine, then fourteen. He began hitting those rising line drives for which he later became famous, and he started driving in runs. But that wasn't all. He also ran the bases with reckless abandon—stealing 17 in 21 attempts.

There was no longer any doubt about it. Cesar Cedeno was right where he belonged: in the big leagues. In the 90 games he played with the Astros, Cesar hit .310, belting out 7 homers, 42 RBI's and 21 doubles. Altogether, he accumulated 110 hits in 355 times at bat.

And Cesar was just as impressive in the field. Making only seven errors in 212 total chances, he racked up a respectable .968 fielding average.

Even with his great performances, Cesar was not voted Rookie of the Year. "We brought him up too

In the 1973 All-Star game, Cedeno raced all the way to the wall on a
drive by Reggie Jackson. But the ball (at left) gets away.

late," said Astro manager Harry Walker, explaining Cesar's failure to win the award. "Not enough of the sportswriters had a chance to see him more than once or twice." (It's the sportswriters who choose the Rookie of the Year.)

Walker, who had been a great hitter himself, was sympathetic to Cedeno. "It wasn't easy for him, you know. He had a language problem, he wasn't home, he's excitable and nervous and sensitive. And he was just a kid. He made some mistakes any rookie will make, but I never saw any youngster with so much raw ability."

By 1971, Cedeno was feeling more comfortable in his surroundings, but he also fell victim to a mild case of the "Sophomore Jinx." His average dropped off to .264. Still, he hit ten home runs and nearly doubled his RBI total, driving in 81 runs. He led the league with 40 doubles and fielded .989, committing just four errors in 354 chances.

In short, Cesar Cedeno became a force to be reckoned with. No one knew that better than Ferguson Jenkins. In one 1971 game when Jenkins was pitching for Chicago, Cedeno used his varied skills to totally frustrate the Cub ace.

First Cesar beat out an infield hit. Then he began to dance and skip around the basepaths. Jenkins, too distracted to concentrate on hitters, walked the next two batters to load the bases.

Now Cedeno was on third, and Jenkins was really

Cesar heads for first after bunting in a 1973 game against the Atlanta Braves. The ball is just above his head.

rattled. Cesar faked a steal of home . . . and it was a superb fake. Jenkins rushed his next pitch, which was wild. Cesar Cedeno scored the winning run.

"What's great about having a player like Cesar on your team," Durocher explained, "is that even if he's in a slump he can still be a threat as a base-stealer, or in the field, or he can get on by bunting. He can do so many things there's no way to shut him off."

There were no slumps for Cedeno in 1972, though. In his third year as a major leaguer, his batting average skyrocketed to .320. His 55 stolen bases set a team record. And, of course, there were all those homers, hits and RBI's that prompted Durocher to compare him to Mays.

Not surprisingly, Cedeno was elected to the 1972 All-Star team, where he contributed one hit and one run scored in two chances at bat. The following year he was on the team again, this time as a starter. Cesar already had 35 stolen bases by the 1973 All-Star break, and he finished the season with 56. His other statistics included 168 hits, 70 RBI's and a super .320 batting average along with 25 homers.

Cesar had come a long way from his boyhood in Santo Domingo. Whether he would admit to it or not, the man he was chasing was named Willie Mays. And Leo Durocher—the man who was in the best position to know—thought Cesar Cedeno could do it.

CATFISH HUNTER

In 1971 everyone was talking about Vida Blue, the Oakland Athletics' sensational rookie pitcher. He won 24 games and several post-season awards that year. Meanwhile, his teammate Jim "Catfish" Hunter had 21 victories—and almost no one noticed.

In 1972, Blue won only six games. Catfish Hunter won another 21. Yet the big question was why Blue *didn't* win 20 games, not why Catfish Hunter did.

Year after year, Catfish was there—reliable, steady, quiet and undramatic.

He didn't throw the ball very hard, for instance— yet he always got his share of strikeouts.

With his pudgy cheeks and friendly smile, he

didn't look very menacing—yet even the best sluggers respected his strong arm.

And of course he never jumped up and down on the mound or yelled at the umpires. All he did was wind up his right arm, kick out his left leg, throw the ball to the catcher—and win another game.

"What he does best," summed up manager Dick Williams, "is win games. He sure does win them, doesn't he?"

In other words, Catfish never did anything that looked very spectacular. But as the Oakland A's got better and better, it suddenly occured to people that Hunter had been spectacular all along.

"I haven't changed at all," Hunter said. "I throw the ball the same way I did in high school. I'm the same pitcher now, except I added a slider since then, and my control is better. But I don't do anything different."

Hunter was just as consistent off the field as on it. Even after the biggest moment of his career Catfish was as reserved and quiet as ever. On May 8, 1968, he pitched a perfect game. Not just a no-hitter, but a perfect game—the eleventh one in the entire history of baseball.

When his jubilant teammates tried to lift him up on their shoulders for a victory ride off the field, Catfish protested. He would have preferred to walk off the field by himself. "I didn't want any more fuss," he explained. "I just wanted to get out of there quick. I was embarrassed."

James Augustus Hunter was born in Hertford, North Carolina, on April 8, 1946. He was the youngest of five sons.

It wasn't until he was six or seven years old that Jim was nicknamed "Catfish." "I ran away from home once," Hunter explained, "and when my folks found me I was sittin' by a stream with a string of catfish next to me. I didn't really want to run away, so I went fishin'."

Hertford was a small, rural town, about 50 miles from Norfolk, Virginia. While no one in the Hunter family ever wanted for meals or winter clothing, they all had to work hard.

"I can remember loading watermelons on trucks for twelve hours a day when I was a teenager," Catfish said. "And I did all the other things kids in my area did. I worked on the farm and I hunted and fished and played sports. I wouldn't have changed my boyhood years for anything."

Catfish went to Perquimans High School in Hertford where he lettered in baseball, football and track. Even then, baseball was his number one sport. But athletics weren't the only thing in Hunter's life—there was always the farm. He would often get up at 4 A.M. to milk the cows, and he had evening chores to do after classes and baseball.

Between Hunter's junior and senior high school years an accident almost ended his athletic career. Jim and one of his brothers had gone hunting, and his brother's shotgun accidentally went off. The small toe of Catfish's right foot was blown off, and a whole load of pellets penetrated his foot.

The town doctor removed about 50 pieces of buckshot right away and then kept taking out more all winter as they worked their way to the surface. The doctor never did get all of them out.

"I laid off everything for the rest of the winter," Hunter remembered, "and I spent a lot of time on crutches. I was worried about being able to pitch again, but it worked out.

"I never could throw as hard as I used to, because of all the time I had to spend on crutches," he continued. "But it didn't hurt my pitchin' that much."

It certainly didn't! Catfish came back to pitch during his senior year and put together a spectacular 14–1 record. That was a fitting ending to a high school career which had included five no-hitters— four of them perfect games.

Not surprisingly, the big league scouts came out in full force. "I remember a game when I struck out twenty-nine men in twelve innings," Catfish said. "I kinda thought those scouts would be interested in that."

So the scouts came often and in ever-larger numbers. And then along came Charley Finley.

Finley was the owner of the Kansas City Athletics, as the team was known before its move to Oakland in 1968. He was a multi-millionaire who owned an insurance company. And he had some unusual ideas about major league baseball.

Finley redesigned the A's uniforms, changing the standard whites and grays to gaudy green and gold. He also tried to convince the league to use orange baseballs, red bases and purple bats—anything to make the game more "colorful" and attract fans into the parks.

"I had never heard of him or the Kansas City Athletics," Hunter recalled, "until one day he pulled into town in a big, black limousine with a motor-cycle escort. Nothing like that had ever happened in Hertford before.

"He put his arm around me and started handing out jackets and bats to everybody, and the other scouts started thinkin' he had me all signed up. So they stayed away."

Finley knew how to get what he wanted—but so did Hunter. Using his country wiles, Catfish kept raising his demands and finally got Finley to pay him $75,000 to sign. But Finley did balk at giving Hunter the new car he wanted.

"He was ready to cancel the whole deal if I held out for the new car, too," Catfish said. "I was kinda dumb. I should have asked him for $80,000. That way I could have had $75,000 and bought my own new car."

Anyway, Catfish signed with the A's, and Finley immediately sent him to the famed Mayo Clinic for another foot operation. Then Hunter went to Finley's farm-estate in LaPorte, Indiana, to recuperate.

Catfish spent the entire 1964 season on the disabled list. Although he didn't pitch at all, he was assigned to the Daytona Beach team in the Florida State League.

In 1965, he was healed and healthy. Normally, the A's would have then sent him to the minors for a year or two of experience. But Hunter had been a bonus player. And in those years bonus players had to spend their first active year on the major league roster or risk being drafted by another team.

So Catfish just sat on the Kansas City bench until mid-season, when an injury to another pitcher forced him into the rotation. Then he compiled an 8–8 record with 82 strikeouts and a 4.26 earned run average in 133 innings. Those were fine statistics for any rookie. But for one who had gone straight from high school to the majors with no minor league seasoning, they were truly impressive.

The following season, 1966, Hunter had nine wins and eleven losses. In 177 innings, he struck out 103 batters and lowered his earned run average to 4.02. From then on, nobody even thought about sending him to the minor leagues.

In 1965, rookie Catfish Hunter pitches for the Athletics (then in Kansas City). He was only 19 years old.

In 1967, Hunter appeared in his first All-Star game (he had been selected for the staff in '66 but saw no action). He finished the season with 13 wins against 17 losses for a team that finished last in a ten-team race, nearly 30 games out of first place. Catfish also chalked up five shutouts, 196 strikeouts and a splendid 2.80 earned run average.

Before the 1968 season began, the Athletics had moved to Oakland. For Hunter, the highlight of '68 came early in the season—May 8, to be exact. That's when he pitched his perfect game against the Minnesota Twins.

As usual, Catfish made it all look simple. There were only two really tense moments in the game. The first came when the Twins' Bob Allison hit a deep grounder. But third-baseman Sal Bando made a difficult fielding play to preserve Hunter's perfect game.

The second rough spot came with two out in the ninth. Batter Rich Reese just wouldn't give up, fouling off five pitches in a row. Hunter was so close to a perfect game. Would Reese spoil it by hitting or forcing a walk? Catfish finally threw him a clean strike to end the game.

"I had good stuff," Hunter recalled. "I could feel that. My fast ball was good all night, which is unusual, and my breaking pitches were sharp. I was happy with my hitting, too. I dropped a bunt in the seventh inning and then in the eighth I got a bases-loaded double to drive in three runs."

It was quite a performance. Catfish had not only pitched a perfect game—he had driven in all the runs in the A's 4–0 victory. Then, to ice the cake, Finley gave Catfish a $5,000 bonus after the game in the team clubhouse.

Catfish ended that season with a 13–13 record, a 3.35 ERA and 172 strikeouts. The Athletics finished sixth of ten teams, but they were improving. Young Reggie Jackson had joined the team, and pitcher Blue Moon Odom had his first big year. Bert Campaneris and Sal Bando were becoming stars. The A's were building a championship club.

In 1969, Catfish was 12–15 with 150 strikeouts and another 3.35 ERA. In 1970 he had another All-Star year. He improved his record to 18–14 and had a 3.81 ERA and 178 strikeouts.

In 1971 the A's won the American League's Western Division championship but lost to Baltimore in the playoffs. That was Vida Blue's big year, but Hunter's 21–11 season was a classic, too. Catfish had a 2.96 ERA and struck out 181 men in 274 innings.

In 1972, Catfish won another 21 games, but this time he lost just seven. He led the team in innings pitched (295), strikeouts (191) and earned run average (2.04). He also pitched 16 complete games and five shutouts.

Oakland finished first in the West Division, then won the American League pennant (beating Detroit in five playoff games). In the playoffs Catfish worked

The scoreboard shows no runs for Minnesota as Hunter walks off the mound after the ninth inning on May 8, 1968. . . .

. . . He had pitched a perfect game, and his excited teammates try to carry the reluctant hero off the field on their shoulders.

$15\frac{1}{3}$ innings, struck out nine men and allowed only two runs, for a 1.17 ERA.

Then the A's met the Cincinnati Reds in the World Series, and Catfish Hunter continued his winning ways.

"We knew he was their ace," said Cincinnati's Johnny Bench. "He sure was super."

Catfish started two games against Cincinnati—and won them both. Altogether, he pitched 16 innings, coming out for a relief man in the ninth inning of each game. He had a fine 2.81 ERA for the Series, allowing only a dozen hits and five earned runs.

After a seven-game cliff-hanger the A's took the Series. In a rare moment of public emotion, Hunter described his feelings.

"It was the end of a long road," he said. "All my professional career I wanted to be on a championship team. I wanted to feel that championship ring on my finger. And I finally got to feel it. I just don't think my life could have been any better."

Catfish, a winter hero in Hertford, tried to "stay out of town because I didn't like people makin' a fuss over me." He hunted and fished, worked at training his 20 hunting dogs—and waited for baseball time to roll around again.

"It's a life I like," he said, "and I came closer to another goal, having my own farm . . . but not to be a dirt farmer, just a gentleman farmer like Mister Finley."

Catfish pitches to Cincinnati's Pete Rose in the 1972 World Series. Hunter started—and won—two games, and the A's won the Series.

Catfish considered his job the easiest and happiest in the world. "Baseball isn't hard work," he said. "Besides, if a pitcher is really overworked, he gets to work maybe forty days a year. Sometimes I get to feelin' guilty, like I'm not doing my share of the work. I wouldn't have it any other way."

Yet the 1973 season started out badly for Catfish. He didn't get his first win until his sixth start. But then he put together a stupendous streak. He won four games in a row before he lost another. Then he strung out 14 more victories before his next loss, which didn't come until mid-September.

Making his streak even more amazing was the fact that in the July 24th All-Star game he had fractured his right thumb trying to stop a smash hit.

Hunter missed two weeks of work, or roughly four starting assignments. It was the first time since 1966 that he had missed his regular turn in the rotation.

"It was a freak accident," he said while recuperating. "It could have happened any time. I think the rest will do me good. I'll be more able to put out in September, when we have our pennant race."

True to his word, Hunter didn't let the injury prevent him from helping Oakland clinch its third straight Western Division championship—or from getting his third 20-game season in a row. Hunter's regular season statistics included a 21–5 record and 3.34 earned run average.

By playoff time Hunter was in fine shape. He won

two games, including the clincher, against the Baltimore Orioles, helping Oakland to the American League pennant. In the World Series he picked up another victory as the A's overcame the New York Mets to capture their second straight championship.

Dave Duncan, who caught for the A's before he was traded to Cleveland in 1973, probably knew Hunter's value better than anyone. According to him, Catfish was one of the easiest pitchers for a catcher to work with.

"He never changed signs," said Duncan. "If he wanted to throw a curve and I called for a fastball, he decided a fastball was the better pitch to throw. He's impossible to get ruffled, and that helps, too. He never comes apart under pressure situations."

Of course not. That would attract attention.

Catfish Hunter once lost a 2–1 game in which he had allowed only three hits. "Even I was bored," he joked. "I'm just not a spectacular kind of player."

Maybe not—but you'd never know it from the records.

NATE COLBERT

Year after year Nate Colbert, an All-Star and a superstar, found himself playing for a last-place team. But the people involved with the cellar-dwelling San Diego Padres agreed they were fortunate to have Nate on their team. They knew that without him things could have been even worse.

In San Diego Nate became known as The Franchise. In professional sports, of course, a franchise is a team. And in the case of the lowly Padres, Nate Colbert *was* their team!

Whenever fans came out to the stadium—which wasn't all that often—the man they came to see was their home run slugging star. And while the team might have let them down, Nate never did.

The 6-foot-2, 210-pounder continued to terrify all the best pitchers in the National League. He earned not only their respect but their "special treatment" as well. As the only real hitting threat in the Padres' line-up, Colbert quickly became the man on whom the pitchers concentrated.

"It's true," admitted Tom Seaver of the New York Mets. "If you can get Nate Colbert out, you can beat the Padres. But there are times when you just can't get him out, or when you'd rather not face him and take a chance. So it's safer to walk him, to put him on first base and then get the next man out."

But even then, Nate Colbert was a hard man to keep down. In 1972, for example, he slugged out 38 homers for a team that won just 58 games. He had 141 hits in 151 games and drove in 111 runs. His .250 batting average was high for a man who had to swing for the fences nearly every time at bat. A base hit wasn't good enough for Nate, for then he would have to rely on another Padre to bring him home—and that wasn't very likely with the weak-hitting San Diego line-up.

All of Nate's efforts were for a team with a 58–95 record, a team 36½ games behind its Western Division champion, Cincinnati, and ten full games behind the next-to-last team in the division. And if that wasn't bad enough, lack of fan interest was causing severe financial problems for the team. Plans were made to move the Padres to Washington, D.C., for the 1974 season.

In 1973, Colbert was still San Diego's only power hitter. He had the added pressure of playing for a team that was planning to move and had to finish out the season in a city that thought it was being abandoned.

"Man, talk about your uncomfortable situations," Nate said with a grin. "There we were, living and playing in San Diego but headed for Washington. I'm not sure if the people wanted us to stay or to leave right away.

"Maybe they even rooted for us to lose. But not too many of them were coming out to the park anyway. Still, the most bothersome thing was the losing. We just couldn't seem to put it together long enough."

Of course Colbert wasn't the only man on the team. There were other promising young players, such as pitcher Steve Arlin, infielder Dave Roberts and outfielders Leron Lee and Clarence Gaston. But the Padres were not strong as a unit, and they continued their losing ways.

"Do I mind the losing? You bet I do," Nate said. "I mind not beating teams I know we could beat. I mind not getting the attention I would get if I played with a strong team. Mostly, I guess, I mind knowing the season is over when there's still months to play. I want to be in the race for a pennant, and I want to play in the World Series."

The Padres had begun as an expansion team in 1969, and after five years in San Diego they still had a long way to go before they could become pennant

Slugger Nate Colbert was a welcome addition to the weak-hitting line-up of the San Diego Padres.

contenders. If they were going to make the most of Nate Colbert's talents, they would have to surround him with other good hitters.

As one opposing pitcher put it, "On another team Nate would have been the most effective clean-up hitter in the league. On a team with a lot of good hitters, how could we pitch around them and then have to face Colbert? What if he hit behind, say, Pete Rose, and ahead of Tony Perez? He'd be murder.

"But with the Padres all we have to do is concentrate on Nate. He's the only one we really worry about, and if he comes up in a bad situation we just walk him."

Nate Colbert was born in St. Louis, Missouri, on April 9, 1946. He quickly learned that major league baseball had played a big part in his father's life, but that was in the Negro major leagues, not what is known today as major league baseball.

Until 1947, when Jackie Robinson broke the racial barrier and played for the Brooklyn Dodgers, no blacks were allowed to play in the major leagues. So the Negro majors provided the only top competition open to blacks. Nate's father, Nathan, had played for the Kansas City Monarchs, one of the best black teams in the country.

"My dad was a pitcher and a catcher," Nate said. "He was always in the action. All during my early years he talked about baseball and I guess it was his love for the game that started my own. I remember him saying that one year the Monarchs played 235 games and he started every one of them. Can you imagine that many games in one season?"

Nate learned baseball strategy from his dad, too. "He just loved to watch any kind of a baseball game," Nate explained. "He'd take me to Busch Stadium and we'd watch while he told me what was really going on. You know, what the players were doing, inside things that most fans didn't know about.

"He would talk all during the game and I learned a lot. But he never made me feel like I had to play. He was just happy to have me along with him. He never pushed baseball on me. If I asked him for advice, he was there to give it. But I made my own decision about playing."

There never was any doubt in Nate's mind that he wanted to be a baseball player. All through high school he continued to play—and to improve. When he graduated and entered St. Louis Baptist College, the major league teams began urging him to sign a contract.

Finally, Nate and his father decided he had better take some of that major league money. It was 1964, before the major league teams had agreed to hold a common draft of players like the pro football teams did. Any team could bid for a highly-regarded young star and the star usually signed with the highest bidder—but not Nate Colbert.

"My dad acted as my negotiator and agent and advisor," Nate remembered. "I guess we had about six or seven offers when I was ready to sign. The best money figure was from the New York Mets, but I was young then, and money didn't mean as much to me. My dad wanted me to sign with St. Louis so he would be able to see me play. I wanted to make him happy, and I took their offer. I just accepted the contract because my father said it was a good one.

"I think I could have gotten more money, but it's not important. You know something? I am sure my dad was more excited than I was when I signed that contract. It was what he had wanted for himself all his life, but he never got the chance. So he was happy for me, because I was getting that chance. It was almost like I was an extension of him."

So Nate Colbert, the third of Nathan Colbert's four sons, set out to become a major leaguer.

Nate's first stop was the Rookie League. He played for the Sarasota, Florida, team as a first baseman and an outfielder. But he was too young and too inexperienced to impress most people. That first season brought Colbert a .217 batting average, two home runs, 18 hits in 45 games and 13 RBI's. It was hardly a sensational year.

But the men who managed the St. Louis farm-team system saw the power and the promise in his natural, fluid swing. So despite his mediocre record they moved him up to Cedar Rapids, Iowa, of the Midwest League in 1965. And there Nate found himself. He learned to smooth out his swing and to hit the curve balls. But even more important, he learned to have confidence in his ability.

"When I was swinging right it didn't matter who was pitching or what kind of a pitch it was," he said. "It still doesn't."

Nate finished the season with 9 homers, 78 hits and 45 RBI's. His batting average climbed to .274. If the Cardinals were impressed, as they certainly should have been, they didn't show it. Each winter a team must list the players it wishes to "protect" from the minor league draft. Those players not on the list are eligible to be bought by another team. The Cardinals decided not to protect Nate, so he was fair game for teams seeking help.

Colbert wasn't surprised at being left unprotected. He was young, and the Cardinals had many promising youngsters in their minor league system. Besides, many teams had been successful in "hiding" players like Nate. But if the Cardinals thought no one would find their raw-boned slugger, they were wrong. The Houston Astros found Nate Colbert and bought his contract.

The Astros kept him on their major league roster all during the 1966 season. But Nate was used only as a pinch hitter and not even very often as that. He appeared at the plate just seven times. Still, it was

major league baseball and major league experience.
That was very important.

"I learned the difference between the way a major
leaguer lives and the dusty bus trips and cold
sandwiches a minor leaguer must accept," said Nate,
remembering that year. "It made me more determined then ever to stay in the majors. No matter
who I played for, I wanted to continue to be a major
leaguer."

But 1967 was to be a minor league year. Nate
played for Amarillo in the Texas League. He had a
fine season: a .293 average, a league-leading 28
homers, 127 hits and 67 RBI's in the 120 games he
played. He also led the league in strikeouts, but
that's not unusual for free-swinging sluggers.

Nate's 1967 performance was enough to move him
up again, this time to Oklahoma City in the Pacific
Coast League. By the time he had 14 home runs and
44 runs batted in, the Astros called him up to the big
leagues. Colbert spent the rest of the 1968 season in
Houston.

Then, on October 14, 1968, Nate Colbert got his
"big break." The Astros, who had been created as an
expansion team in 1962, lost Nate to yet another
expansion team, the brand-new San Diego Padres.

The Padres had been given the chance to draft
players from the other teams in the league, and
Nate—unprotected once more—was the man they
wanted from Houston.

Nate was overjoyed with the move. "I thought it

was going to be my big chance to play regularly. I figured the Padres wouldn't be very good right off, and they'd have to go with younger players like me. That was all I wanted, the chance to play every day. I was tired of sitting on the bench or pinch-hitting or playing half a season in the minor leagues."

Given a steady diet of baseball, Colbert proved to be the big hitter the Padres needed. His first full season as a regular (1969), Nate responded with solid statistics. He batted .255, collecting 24 homers, 66 RBI's and 123 hits.

"He was as good a hitter as I had faced all year," said Tom Seaver, who won the Cy Young Award that season as the National League's outstanding pitcher. "Nate got hold of a few of my best fastballs and really ripped them."

Nate's efforts were impressive enough for him to finish second to Ted Sizemore of the Dodgers in the Rookie of the Year voting. And he followed that fine season with an even better one in 1970.

The Padres had only 63 wins in 1970 against 99 losses. But Nate was superb. He hit 38 home runs. He drove in 86 runs. He batted .259. He had 148 hits. He played in 156 games. And, of course, he established himself as one of the league's top sluggers.

"I thought it was my most important year," he said, "because I had proved the year before was no mistake. I had to face the same pitchers and now

First baseman Colbert waits for the pick-off throw from the pitcher, but a St. Louis base-runner dives back safely.

they knew how they wanted to throw to me. I was concentrating even harder, because if they were able to handle me that year it could have changed my whole career."

Preston Gomez, who managed the Padres for their first three seasons, found himself with a genuine star. "After that 1970 season we all knew what Nate could do," said Gomez. "It was just a matter of him concentrating and us finding enough good players to keep him company. He concentrated, but we didn't hold up our end of the bargain. Nate did more than a player should be asked to do."

In 1971 Nate's average was .264. He hammered out 27 homers, 84 RBI's and 149 hits and was the league's leading first baseman in putouts (1,372). It wasn't surprising that Nate Colbert was named to the National League All-Star team.

"It was a thrill, no doubt about it," he said. "I suppose the All-Star game and the World Series are the two goals every major league player has. I had achieved one of them in my third season. I was proud of myself."

Colbert had good reason to be proud, as he proved in the years that followed. His reputation as a hitter spread, and even Hammerin' Hank Aaron—one of *the* all time great hitters—was impressed. Aaron became a Colbert admirer after the Atlanta super-slugger got an eye-witness view of an amazing Colbert performance.

The Padres' third base coach congratulates Colbert as he heads for home after a home run in 1971.

It was during a doubleheader between the Atlanta Braves and the Padres on August 1, 1972. In the first game of the twin bill, Nate hit three homers and drove in eight runs. In the second game, he racked up two more homers and two singles for five more RBI's. He hit for 22 total bases that day, setting a major league record.

Colbert's 13 runs batted in broke the record for a doubleheader set by Stan Musial. The former Cardinal outfielder had been one of Nate's childhood heroes. And Nate's five home runs had tied another Musial record.

"When I hit the fourth home run I remembered being in Busch Stadium with my dad the day Musial hit those five," Colbert said. "I can remember thinking no one would ever equal that record, certainly not me. But then I did it."

Aaron watched that performance with open-mouthed admiration. "He is just now starting to mature," Hank said. "He is only beginning to emerge as a hitter. Nate didn't swing hard on some of those homers today, but if your swing is grooved you don't have to. That's part of the secret and he's starting to find it out. I think if he played in a park like ours all the time he'd have as much of a chance to hit sixty in a season as any man who ever played."

Nate was pleased with the records, of course, but he was even more satisfied with Aaron's praise.

"I'm not too interested in the record books," Colbert said, "but what I do feel proud of is the respect I started to get that season. I know some people were surprised when I was named to my first All-Star team. I guess maybe they figured the Padres had to have someone on it so it might as well be me. But in my heart I felt I belonged and I have to keep proving I deserve it now, or I won't deserve it."

There was no question that Nate Colbert was indeed a superstar. But unfortunately none of his luster seemed to be rubbing off on the Padres. Nate Colbert's job remained as difficult—and frustrating —as ever.

"I have to be counted on as a power hitter with this team," he said during the 1973 All-Star break. "I always was, and that's all right, but I get down on myself when I'm not producing the way I should and it's unfair for anyone to think I can carry the whole load of the team here.

"On most teams, when a guy hits a slump there's someone else around to pick up the slack. We have those kind of guys now, but I'm just anxious for them to start showing it. It would make me an even better hitter."

Colbert finished the '73 season with 22 homers, 143 hits, 80 RBI's and a .270 batting average. The Padres, on the other hand, wound up with an embarrassing 60–102 record—the worst in the league.

Still, Nate Colbert had accomplished *most* of the goals he had set for himself while still a schoolboy in St. Louis.

"I wanted to make the major leagues," he recalled. "Then I wanted to be a regular and a slugger. I wanted to play in the All-Star Game. There's only one thing left. The World Series."

Nate Colbert had done all that any one man could do. Now the Padres knew it was up to them. After all, Nate Colbert had been World Series quality from the start.

BOBBY MURCER

It takes a special blend of skills to be a major league centerfielder: an ability to run like the wind when chasing down line drives and fly balls, surehandedness and a strong arm for the long throw home. It also takes a certain amount of courage, because a great fielder can't worry about the fences and walls when he's pursuing a well-hit ball.

Bobby Murcer had all that and more.

A centerfielder seldom gets along only on his fielding skills. At bat he must be smart and strong to beat out a bunt one time up and blast the pitcher's best curve ball over the wall the next time.

Bobby Murcer could do that too, and he added a special magic that promised to make him one of baseball's superstars.

"Bobby is the finest centerfielder in the league and one of the best the Yankees have ever had," said manager Ralph Houk. "I'm sure he can be as good as the others, too."

"The others" were Joe DiMaggio and Mickey Mantle, two of the greatest centerfielders in history. Both of them had been Yankees. And it was to them that Bobby Murcer was always compared.

During his 18 years as a Yankee, Mickey Mantle had hit 536 home runs, driven in more than 1,500 runs and maintained a lifetime batting average of .298. Twice he had hit more than 50 home runs in a season, and in 1956 he won the triple crown, leading the league with a .353 average, 130 RBI's and 52 homers. When he retired after the 1968 season, Yankee fans started looking for another superman.

In the spring of 1969 young Bobby Murcer joined the Yankees full-time. His early performances gave fans the hope that another Mantle had arrived on the scene. But Mantle was a tough act to follow, and Bobby resented the comparisons.

"I never felt I had Mickey's ability, and I still don't think I do," he said. "It seemed rather foolish to me to be compared to Mantle and DiMaggio, and it made me very uncomfortable. All I can ever hope for is to be able to play my best every day and help the team win. I don't like to compare myself to anyone."

Murcer was determined to become a star in

The big swing of Bobby Murcer brought to mind the swing of another great Yankee center fielder—Mickey Mantle.

baseball his own way, and he claimed that comparisons with others even held him back by forcing him to go for the home run too often.

But no one could blame the fans for making comparisons—especially between Murcer and Mantle. Both were born and raised in Oklahoma, both had been infielders in the minor leagues, both had been discovered by the same Yankee scout, both found their way to center field in Yankee Stadium. And both had the special something that sets off a star from the rest of the players.

Bobby Ray Murcer was born May 20, 1946, in Oklahoma City. While many star athletes credit their fathers for their interest in sports, Bobby couldn't.

His father had very little interest in sports. "It must have been born in him," Mr. Murcer said of his son's abilities. "Otherwise, I don't know where he developed it. I enjoyed watching games and I liked watching him perform, but I never did follow sports very much."

Nevertheless, Bobby and his two brothers, Dwayne and Randy, grew to love almost all sports. They played not only baseball but football and basketball, too.

Bobby played in the local Pee Wee Leagues from the time he was seven years old, but no one expected him to become a major league star. He was much too small. Later he played ball for Southwest High School in Oklahoma City. But he was still too small. Nobody that size could make it big in sports. "I was a little guy," Murcer recalled. "I was about five-feet-seven-inches, and I don't think I weighed much more than a hundred and five or ten pounds. But I loved to play."

Bobby's coach in high school was a man named Brooks Moser. Murcer played football for Moser as a running back and a linebacker, and he was a shortstop on the baseball team Moser coached.

"I never saw a tougher little guy," Moser remembered later on. "He never backed down from a challenge, and he never let another boy's size be a part of his decision to play aggressively."

Despite his size, Murcer earned All-State honors in both football and baseball. "He had a fine batting eye," coach Moser said, "and he was a leader on the teams, too. The other boys really respected him and his ability. In football, he just played with great courage. Everything he did, it seemed, he did with a thousand percent effort."

By the time Bobby was a senior at Southwest High, several scouts were after him to sign baseball contracts, and many colleges were offering him football and baseball scholarships. His decision to play baseball was partly influenced by Mickey Mantle's reputation.

"All of us in Oklahoma thought of Mickey as a

hero, as an ideal," Bobby explained. "He was a home state boy making it big in New York City. We would follow the newspapers, and we all rooted for the Yankees. I guess that sounded strange way out in Oklahoma, but it was because of Mickey. Also, when the scouts started coming around, I guess I was thinking about him when I decided on the Yankees."

Long before Bobby decided on the Yankees, scout Tom Greenwade had decided on him. Tom had been kept up-to-date on the progress of Murcer's high school and American Legion summertime careers. As soon as Bobby was old enough, Tom came around with a contract.

"We had kept tabs on Bobby for about three years," Greenwade said. "So few kids ever make it to the majors that the teams don't really know who the scouts are scouting. They didn't know Murcer until I recommended him."

Eight major league teams were interested in signing Bobby. The Yanks offered him a $20,000 bonus, and he finally took it although another team had offered even more. "I was just too involved with Mantle and the Yankees," he said.

The signing took place in June of 1964, and Bobby Murcer, as Mickey Mantle before him, became a New York Yankee. But it would be a long time before he became a member of the New York Yankees on the field. Before he got to New York he had a position change, a minor league career, two years in the Army and a baseball "education" to get through.

Murcer's career with the Yankee organization began in Johnson City, Tennessee, in the Appalachian League. Shortly after his high school graduation, Bobby got on a plane for the first time in his life and flew to Tennessee to begin his baseball career.

Bobby had grown to 5-foot-10 and weighed nearly 160 pounds. Although he was still no giant, he was a good size for a young minor league infielder. Starting in mid-season, Bobby played in 32 games for Johnson City. He hit only two home runs, but he had 46 hits in 126 at-bats for a great .365 average. As a second baseman–shortstop Bobby made 34 errors— more than one a game—but no one had any complaints.

Bobby's next stop was Greensboro of the Carolinas League, where in 1965 he became a full-time shortstop and a full-time slugger. It all came together then, as Bobby batted .322 in 126 games and racked up 16 home runs, 90 RBI's and 154 hits. He was still making errors—in fact, he led the league's shortstops with 55—but his steaming bat more than made up for that.

The Yankees were so impressed with Murcer's performance that they called him up to New York near the end of the '65 season. His experience in the majors amounted to just eleven games and 37 chances at the plate, but that was long enough for

Bobby to drive in four runs and get his first major league four-bagger.

"That first home run was special, and I'll never forget it," Bobby said. "It came in Washington off a pitcher named Jim Duckworth, and when I got to home plate there was Mickey Mantle to shake my hand. It was like a dream . . . I couldn't believe it all happened just like that."

It was a good beginning, but it didn't last long. There were many unhappy moments for Bobby and the Yankees during the next few seasons. In the spring of 1966 veteran shortstop Tony Kubek was injured, and Bobby felt the pressure of competing for a starting job.

Murcer stayed with the Yankees through their first 21 games, but he just didn't have enough experience for the big leagues, and the team's officials knew it. So they sent the 19-year-old to their Toledo, Ohio, farm team in the International League.

That was Bobby's last minor league trip, and he made the most of it. He hit .266 with 15 homers, 62 RBI's, and 131 hits. His fielding improved, too, and he participated in 91 double plays, a league-leading total for shortstops.

Then, in 1967 and 1968, he had to stay out of baseball entirely when he was drafted by the United States Army. In October of 1967 he had applied for acceptance by a unit of the Army Reserves. Most athletes tried for that, since it meant losing only two

Bobby is tagged in the stomach by Washington's Paul Casanova in a 1969 game. But Murcer drove in four runs and the Yanks won.

weeks every summer. While waiting to be admitted to the unit, Bobby and his girl, Kay Rhodes of Oklahoma City, were married. Then a letter came from the Army—but it was a draft notice.

The Yankees were as disappointed as Murcer, but there was no choice. So instead of going to Florida for spring training, Bobby went to Fort Bliss, Texas, for basic training. Then he was shipped to Fort Huachua in Arizona, where he stayed until his discharge nearly two years later.

Meanwhile, the Yankees were floundering. In 1967 they had finished with a 72–90 record, ninth in what was then a ten-team American League. The following year they showed some improvement with an 83–79 mark, and by the time Bobby got his army discharge in 1969, the Yankees were on the rise again.

Army life, or maybe just two years of growth, had made Murcer bigger. He was a hefty 190 pounds now, and had grown to 5-foot-11. The new strength showed. He hit the ball harder, and with more distance, than ever before.

As a regular for the first time, Bobby had a satisfying season. Opening day of 1969 found the Yankees in Washington against the Senators (who later became the Texas Rangers). Bobby slammed a "tape-measure" home run.

The next day he hit another one, almost as long. Then, when the Yankees came back to New York, he continued his super-slugging. In the first game of the season in Yankee Stadium, he hit a home run (his third), a double and a single.

The next day he hit another home run, and he followed that up with still another the next day. In the Yankees' first nine games, Bobby Murcer had hit five home runs!

By mid-May Bobby was near the top of the league with his .324 batting average, and his ten home runs and 38 RBI's led the majors. The fans were sure they had seen the beginning of another "Mickey Mantle" legend.

But then Murcer lost his swing. And then he injured the heel of his left foot. And then he began to make errors at third base . . . four in one game, in fact.

And he lost his confidence.

"It seemed like nothing went right, after nothing had gone wrong," Bobby recalled. "I couldn't handle the grounders at third, and I was missing pitches I should have hit over the fence. Even when I hit a ball good, it was right at someone who caught it."

For the two months of June and July, Bobby Murcer managed just two more home runs. But it was, in all, a satisfactory season. Bobby wound up with 26 home runs, 82 RBI's and a .259 average. He drew several Rookie of the Year votes.

One of Bobby's problems—his infield errors—was solved by Manager Ralph Houk, who had moved him from third base to right field in the latter part of the '69 season. Houk later announced that Bobby would be the new centerfielder for 1970.

Being away from third base worked out fine, and Bobby regained his hitting touch in 1970. Then came June 24 in New York, when the Yankees were playing a doubleheader with the Cleveland Indians.

In his last at-bat in the first game, Bobby hit a home run. In his first time up in the second game, he hit another. Then another. And still another to tie the major league record of four consecutive home runs.

With the help of Bobby Murcer, the Yankees were looking better and better. But their charge at the pennant fell short, and they finished second to Baltimore. Still, they had a magnificent 93–69 record, and Bobby wound up with some fine statistics of his own: 23 homers, 82 RBI's, 146 hits and a .251 average.

Now he was on the way. In 1971 his statistics were even more impressive. He finished the season with 25 home runs, 94 RBI's, 175 hits and a torrid .331 average. That performance earned him his first selection to the All-Star team, as the starting centerfielder.

Murcer duplicated that honor the following year —but he did it the hard way. He got off to a slow start with another batting slump, and by the end of May he was batting a dismal .206. One month later he had brought his average up to .264. By the end of the season he had an impressive .292 average, with 33 homers, 96 RBI's and 171 hits.

In 1973, Bobby made the All-Star team for the third year in a row, pulling in more votes than any American League outfielder. This time he finished the season with 22 home runs, 95 RBI's, 187 hits and a fine .304 batting average. At the age of 26, he was already being recognized as one of the best sluggers in the major leagues.

"Bobby has made amazing progress," said Baltimore's star pitcher Dave McNally. "He used to chase all the high fast balls and I could get him out without throwing a strike. I can remember throwing to him neck-high and nose-high. But now he has more discipline. Now he waits, and when he gets the pitch he wants, look out."

Hall of Fame member Ted Williams, perhaps the finest hitter in the history of the game, was another of Murcer's fans. "He's got all the tools he needs," said Williams. "Good wrists, good shoulders, a fine eye. He can't miss now."

No more comparisons for Bobby Murcer. He was finally on his own. And who knows, maybe some day—say in 1985—Yankee fans will see a rookie centerfielder and they'll nod their heads and say, "He looks like the new Bobby Murcer, doesn't he?"

JOHN MAYBERRY

In December of 1971 John Mayberry joined the Kansas City Royals. He came from the Houston Astros in exchange for two minor-league pitchers, and the trade hardly made headlines, even in Kansas City. Those who did read about the trade must have asked, who is John Mayberry?

Mayberry was nearly a nobody. He had spent five years in the Houston farm system, and for a while he had been considered a promising first baseman. But in 1971 he had appeared in 46 major-league games for the Astros and achieved a miserable .182 batting average. So the Houston team gave up and traded him.

Kansas City fans hardly expected the newcomer

to make a big difference to their team in 1972. By the end of the season, however, they knew their team had made the trade of the year. In his first full major league season, young Mayberry hit .298, drove in 100 runs and hit 25 homers. Suddenly he was being acclaimed as one of the most promising young stars in the game. The up-and-coming Royals had an up-and-coming slugger.

Back in Houston, the first baseman for 1972 was veteran Lee May who had been obtained in a costly trade. Houston fans could have cried when they discovered that even the highly rated May didn't have as good a season as Mayberry. The Astros glumly agreed that they had given up on the young first baseman one season too early. It seemed that they could hear the cheers all the way from Kansas City.

Big John Mayberry was born February 18, 1950, in Detroit. He went to Northwestern High School which had already produced such fine athletes as the Tigers' Willie Horton, former American League batting champ Alex Johnson and his football-playing brother Ron.

"I played baseball and basketball, but I was too scared to play football," Mayberry joked. "Besides, the way I played, two sports were enough to keep me busy all year."

Actually, John was equally good at both sports. In

fact, in one high school basketball game he out-
scored Ralph Simpson, who went on to play with the
ABA's Denver Rockets.

Graduation time brought John face-to-face with a
big decision. Michigan State offered him an athletic
scholarship, and the Houston Astros made him their
number one draft choice. To help him make up his
mind, the Astros offered Mayberry a reported
$30,000 bonus to sign with them.

"I could have accepted the scholarship to Michigan State," John said, "or I could have taken the
Houston money. I took the money."

So in 1967 the 17-year-old first baseman headed
for Covington, Kentucky, the Astros' rookie farm
team in the Appalachian League. There he picked
up 4 homers, 21 RBI's, and a .252 batting average.

"I was finding out what organized baseball was
like," he said. "I needed some time to learn."

In 1968, John learned a lot of things—in a lot of
different places. He started the season with the
Cocoa team of the Class A Florida State League,
where he hit .338 with 48 RBI's and 14 homers.
Then he was sent to the Carolinas League's Greensboro club. There he hit .329, drove in 29 runs and
belted out 8 round-trippers. After a brief stint with
the triple-A Oklahoma City team, Mayberry was
brought up to Houston for the last few weeks of the
season.

All told, his minor league statistics included 23

Playing first base for Houston, John Mayberry holds a Cincinnati base-runner close to the bag.

homers and 82 RBI's. But in nine at-bats with the Astros, Mayberry failed to get a hit.

The Astros knew they had a power hitter in John Mayberry, but they weren't sure he was ready for a steady diet of major league pitching. So for the next two years John commuted between Oklahoma City and Houston.

In 1969 he played in 123 games for the Oklahoma team, hitting .303 with 21 homers, 78 RBI's and 139 hits in 458 at-bats. Again he was brought up to Houston near the end of the season. He made brief appearances in five Astro games, and after four times at bat, he was still looking for his first major-league hit.

Although Mayberry found the constant commuting unsettling, there were some exciting moments during that year. In one of his early appearances in Houston, John was playing first base when he found himself face-to-face with the great Henry Aaron.

"The Hammer got a single and there he was, just standing there on the bag," Mayberry recalled. "The pitcher threw over to me to keep the Hammer close, and I swiped my glove at him. Then I threw it back. Then I thought, 'this is the Hammer. This is Henry Aaron!' I yelled for the pitcher to throw the ball back again because I just wanted to touch him once more."

In 1970, Mayberry spent a lot more time in Houston, but he was still far from being a regular.

Mayberry scores for the Astros as Giant pitcher Gaylord Perry drops the throw. The ball is just behind Mayberry's leg.

"I didn't like all the traveling back and forth," he said. "I played with Oklahoma City and practiced with the Astros. Then I'd play with the Astros and get things going good and they'd send me back to Oklahoma City."

The 1970 statistics show that Mayberry was a consistent slugger in the high minor league. In 70 Oklahoma City games he hit .273, drove in 38 runs and added 13 homers to his total. In his 50 games with the Astros, however, his statistics reflected the tougher competition. Although he did collect five homers and fourteen RBI's in Houston, his batting average dropped to .216.

"Lots of times I'd get in the game late, for defense," he explained. "I just didn't have the chance to get into a routine. I must say it was not the best way to try to play."

By 1971 the Astros knew they had to make a decision about their promising first baseman. Other teams were beginning to look at Mayberry with interest, and the Astros still weren't sure that John could make it in the majors.

So that year the Astros watched as he played— again—in both Oklahoma City and Houston. But although his Oklahoma City statistics were great, once more his Astro efforts were meager.

The Houston management decided to make the move. They began answering those teams that called to inquire about Mayberry, and they started looking for another first baseman. Finally, they acquired Lee May from the Cincinnati Reds.

"When they got May, I knew I was gone," said John.

So when Mayberry was traded to the Kansas City Royals he was disappointed but not surprised. That disappointment didn't last long, however, as it soon became clear that the Royals had big plans for John.

Cedric Tallis, general manager of the Royals and a keen judge of talent, had been anxious to get Mayberry for a long time. "He has all the ingredients for greatness," Tallis said. "First of all he is a fine person with a great attitude. He also has the necessary physical skills to become one of the great stars of baseball for many years."

Equally impressed with Mayberry was Kansas City scout Bob Lemon. "I've never seen anybody as good as he is at his age for knowing the strike zone," Lemon said.

"Most big swingers have no idea what a strike is at that age. They learn it, but it's usually when they're three or four years older."

Mayberry, getting his first full chance in the major leagues, made the most of it. He got off to a fine start in 1972, hitting safely in his first seven games and in eleven of his first twelve, for a .318 average.

A late spring slump dropped him to a season low of .205, but he came out of it stronger than ever. During the month of June he drove in 30 runs and

smashed 6 homers. During one stretch he hit safely
in 14 straight games (and got five of his six homers
for the month). Then after one hitless game he hit
safely in six more, making it 20 of 21 games overall.
By that time his batting average was over .300.

Later in the season Mayberry hit four home runs
in four consecutive games against the New York
Yankees. He wrapped up the season with a fantastic
September streak during which he hit nine more
homers.

On September 20 in California he hit his first
major league grand slam home run, off the Angels'
Rudy May, and during that same road trip he got a
pair of three-run homers off Oakland's Vida Blue.

The second three-run blast gave John his 100th
RBI, and that made him only the third man in
baseball history to reach that figure in his first full
season. (The other two were Willie Horton and
Willie Mays.)

It was hard to believe that the Kansas City
super-slugger was the same man who had so little
success in Houston just a year ago. Even Mayberry
had trouble explaining the big change.

"I think the big difference between Houston and
Kansas City," he said, "is that I was told the job was
mine with the Royals. Even when I was in a slump, I
didn't have to worry about being benched. They told
me I was their first baseman no matter what. That's
an unbelievable situation. I loved it."

And Kansas City loved John Mayberry! The Royals were in the pennant race for most of 1972, and manager Jack McKeon was amazed at the poise and leadership shown by his young star.

"The pitchers worked around him, and he still remained a great pressure hitter," McKeon said. "He'd get bad pitches, and he'd stay off them—or he'd get pitches that most kids would be tempted to try to pull, but he'd just hit 'em where they were pitched for singles."

Despite Mayberry's big bat, however, the Royals fell short of the pennant in '72. In 1973, John really started steaming. By All-Star time, he was at the top of the league with an incredible 80 RBI's and 20 homers. There was no doubt that John Mayberry was truly an All-Star.

Oakland's Dick Williams, who was managing the American League's team, said, "I'd have to be crazy to leave him off the team when the game is being played in Kansas City. The people here would kill me."

Actually, Mayberry was automatically on the team. He finished second to Chicago's Dick Allen in the national voting for first baseman. And when Allen broke his leg before the game, Mayberry became the first-base starter.

"I didn't even think I'd make the squad," Mayberry said, "and now I'm starting. It's a real honor to play in this game."

After he was traded to the Kansas City Royals, Big John's big swing made him a star.

John was the only starter for either league without prior All-Star game experience, but he wasn't at all nervous.

"I had enough of a struggle to make the major leagues to be upset by one game," he explained. "It's really just another game. You get three strikes here, too, even though it is the All-Star game."

The American League lost the game, 7–1, but Mayberry got one of the five hits the squad managed to collect.

During the second half of the season John fell into his first big slump. But he still finished with a .278 average and 26 homers. And for the second straight season he had 100 or more RBI's.

After two years in the majors, it seemed certain that John Mayberry's travels were over. No more would he see Oklahoma City—or any place else that wasn't big league.

With his heavy bat, John would be intimidating catchers and pitchers for years to come.

"He's going to be one of the very great hitters," said Boston pitcher John Curtis. "He has that big swing, but he knows what he's doing. His size is certainly important, but that big swing of his is even more frightening to a pitcher. He can hit any pitch out of the park."

Bill Lee, Boston's outstanding relief specialist, preferred to joke away the major threat posed by

John Mayberry. When asked how he would pitch to Mayberry, Lee once answered:

"I'm not sure. Let me see first which way the wind is blowing."

As much as he enjoyed the praise, John always tried to change the subject when the word "superstar" came up.

"I don't know what to say," he admitted. "I don't even think about things like that. I'm a lucky guy who got traded to the right team at the right time. I'm playing a game I love, making some money and having some fun."

Money seemed to be the least of it. John didn't even spend the $30,000 the Astros paid him to sign.

"I just put it away," he said. "I just saved it for a rainy day."

To most people, a "rainy day" means a time when they are down on their luck and money is needed. But the way things were going for John Mayberry, the only rainy day he'd have to worry about was the kind that meant a game would be postponed.

CARLTON FISK

"I got a late start in the majors," said Boston catcher Carlton Fisk after his first full year of play. "I had to do everything in a hurry."

Fisk considered himself an "old rookie" at the age of 25 when he came up to the Red Sox to stay in 1972. He felt he had to make up for all the time he had lost in minor league towns like Greenville (North Carolina), Waterloo (Iowa), Pittsfield (Massachusetts) and Pawtucket (Rhode Island).

He did make up for lost time—with one of the best rookie seasons on record. After less than half a season Fisk was named to the American League's All-Star team. At the end of the year he became the first player ever to be chosen Rookie of the Year by a unanimous vote, and one of the few to win a Gold Glove award for having the best fielding record at his position.

Statistically, the record clearly spoke out for Carlton Fisk. In 1972 he hit 22 home runs, more than any American League catcher. His .293 batting average was the highest on the Red Sox, the highest among all the league's catchers and the ninth highest in the league. In 131 games he had 61 RBI's and 134 hits, including 28 doubles and a league-leading 9 triples.

It was an unbelievable beginning for the super-rookie. His outstanding major league debut so impressed the Boston fans and sportswriters that they voted him the most valuable player on the team. In fact, the only one who didn't find anything unusual about his instant stardom was Fisk himself.

"I've always been an All-Star," the outspoken catcher stated. "It just took time before everybody else got to realize it."

What did he think about having more home runs than any Red Sox catcher in history? "I was surprised it wasn't more than just twenty-two," he said.

And how about his place on the All-Star team? "Like I said, I felt I should have been there all along, but it did feel good to know there wasn't another rookie on the squad. And it did feel good to get to play. But it felt better the next year (1973) when I was voted to start the game."

**Carlton Fisk holds his ground as Cleveland's Chris Chambliss
crashes into home plate in 1972. Fisk was a rookie with Boston.**

Carlton was just as blunt about his teammates. He quickly became a team leader and felt confident enough to criticize other stars on the team when he felt they weren't playing their best.

"I always felt that anybody who wanted to criticize another player better have the record on his side," Fisk said. "When I felt I did, there was no feeling of reluctance. I felt it was my job. After all, we were in the pennant race until the last day of the season."

Carlton Ernest Fisk was born December 26, 1947, in Bellows Falls, Vermont, but he grew up right across the state line in Charlestown, New Hampshire, a tiny New England town of 1,600 people.

As a boy, Carlton picked up the nickname of "Pudge"—he admits to being "a fat little kid." That nickname followed him to the majors, though at 6-foot-2 and 210 bone-hard pounds he was hardly pudgy.

"I worked off that baby fat by doing chores on the farm," he recalled. "I would milk cows, chop wood, do all the odd jobs. My brothers and I had to do what we were told. It was just the way things were in our family. We had a lot of fun, but we had a lot of work, too."

Nevertheless, Carlton and his three brothers—Cedric, Conrad and Calvin—still found time for baseball, basketball and football. They all played well, as they were expected to, because their father Cecil had been an athletic legend in New Hampshire.

"The older men up home tell me there never was a finer all-around athlete than my father," Carlton said, "and I can remember playing hard all the time, no matter what the score, just to make sure he was pleased with me."

One incident that stood out vividly in Fisk's boyhood memories concerned a high school basketball game in the New Hampshire state championship tournament. It was a semi-final round game, and Carlton's Charlestown High team was favored to win.

"I scored forty points and grabbed thirty-six rebounds, but we lost by three," he recalled.

"After the game, my dad told me I had missed four of six free throws and that if I had made them all my team would have won.

" 'Don't depend on the others to win,' he told me. 'Try to do it yourself. It's a team sport, but the teams with the best individuals win the championships.' "

When he wasn't playing basketball, young Carlton could be found on the baseball field. "In the Little League I was a catcher because nobody else wanted to be," he remembered. "But I had to give it up because I outgrew the equipment, and they had just that one set of stuff, nothing larger.

"In high school I was mainly a pitcher because I could throw hard. Then in American Legion ball I was a shortstop. In fact, my Legion coach told me the only chance I had of making it to the majors was as a shortstop."

When he graduated from Charlestown High, Carlton was offered his choice of a baseball or basketball scholarship to the University of New Hampshire. He chose basketball.

"My hero was always Bill Russell, who played for all those great Boston Celtic teams," Fisk explained. "He was the kind of athlete I admired. He always played to win . . . he knew he was good . . . and he never gave up, but he always played fair. I would have loved to play professional basketball except I just wasn't quick enough to be a guard and I was too short for any other position in the pros.

"It was in college that I realized I wasn't pro basketball material, especially when those six-foot-eight-inch forwards stuffed the ball back in my face when I shot. At the same time I was playing a lot of sandlot baseball, and when the Red Sox offered me a contract in 1967, I took it."

But Carlton found out that Boston didn't want him as a pitcher or as a shortstop. He was asked to catch. That was all right with Fisk. Like his father, he was a natural athlete, and his early catching savvy soon came rushing back to him.

After signing with the Red Sox, on February 3, 1967, Carlton reported to Greenville (North Carolina) but was immediately drafted by the U.S. Army and spent 1967 in the service.

His first minor league team was Waterloo, where he hit .338 with 12 home runs, 34 RBI's and 66 hits in just 62 games.

That was too good for the Midwest League, so the Red Sox moved him up to Pittsfield of the Eastern League for 1969. Again he had a strong season, hitting .243 with 41 RBI's, 18 doubles and 10 homers. As a reward, Carlton was brought up to Boston for the final few days of the American League season. As a member of the Red Sox he only got to bat five times and didn't get a hit.

In 1970, Fisk was back in the Eastern League, this time with Pawtucket. His rapid progress as a catcher continued, and his hitting never faltered.

Throughout his minor league years Fisk showed the ability—and the attitude—of a champion. Darrell Johnson, one of Carlton's minor league managers, was particularly impressed with the young catcher's determination.

"I remember one day when he was hit by a pitch," said Johnson. "His nose was broken in four places, and when the ball hit him he dropped as though somebody had knocked him out. I ran to the plate and asked if he could hear me, if he was all right. He just jumped up, blood pouring from his nose, and took his stance in the batter's box again. I knew he was a tough kid."

Johnson was the man Carlton found most helpful in his professional career. In fact, he often compared the former major league catcher to his father. "Both men had a lot to do with my success," he said. "My dad taught me to be tough and to play hard. Darrell taught me to think about all the important facets of the catcher's job, the things that help the pitchers. Like the fundamentals, backing up first base on a grounder, covering third on bunts, hustling all the time to show the other guys you really want to play ball."

More technically, Johnson taught Fisk how to separate his two jobs—catching and hitting. "He showed me that baseball is made up of offense and defense," said Fisk. "And he trained me to think of each part separately."

Until then, Fisk had been having problems with his concentration. At bat, he would worry about a passed ball he made or a hit a batter got because he had called for the wrong pitch. But Johnson taught him to keep his mind on hitting only. Behind the plate, however, Carlton had to force himself to stop worrying about his hitting and concentrate strictly on helping the pitcher get the batters out, playing top defense, running the game.

By 1971, Fisk was being hailed as a future star in Boston. That season he was sent to Louisville of the International League for some more experience. Bingo! He hit .263. He drove in 43 runs. He slammed out 10 homers, had 81 hits and showed everyone that he was ready for the majors.

Again he was sent to the Red Sox for the final

Once he learned to separate his two jobs—catching and hitting—Fisk became a big threat at the plate.

weeks of the season. He appeared in 14 games, picking up 15 hits in 48 at-bats. And this time he was determined to stay. "I'm not sure what anybody else felt," he stated, "but I was not about to leave the team again. I had had enough of the minor leagues."

Red Sox manager Eddie Kasko was one of Carlton's biggest fans. "You could just see how hard he played, how much he wanted to win. It's difficult to keep those kind of guys on the bench, much less in the minor leagues. All Pudge needed was the confidence to hit major league pitching. Privately, I had counted on him to be the regular catcher in 1972, but he surprised even me with how well he played."

When Carlton was chosen to the All-Star team halfway through his first full season, the rest of the league was stunned, and even his fans were surprised. Fisk accepted the honor with his usual bravado.

But when Carlton actually found himself on the field, he had a different reaction altogether. "Imagine, I was out there with guys like Hank Aaron and Willie Mays," he said. "When I got in the game and they came up to hit, I just couldn't help thinking about when I was a kid and collecting their bubble gum cards.

"I was really nervous when Bill Freehan caught the first five innings and I took his place in the sixth. How nervous? Well, I figured he had caught the first six innings, so that I was in for the seventh. Well, Gaylord Perry of the Indians came in when I did and he pitched two innings. Then Wilbur Wood of the White Sox replaced him and when Wilbur got them out in the bottom of the eighth—with us ahead,

3–2—I figured it was the bottom of the ninth and we had just won the game.

"I ran out, shook his hand and said, 'Atta boy, Wilbur, way to go!' He looked at me as if I was really nuts. It's not hard to imagine how embarrassed I was when he said we had another inning to go."

In 1973, Fisk proved that his phenomenal rookie season had not been a fluke. This time he played in 135 games, and although his batting average dropped to .246, he wound up with 26 home runs, 125 hits and 71 RBI's.

Carlton was by no means Superman, though, and as a hitter he had his problems with certain opposing pitchers. Take Nolan Ryan, for instance.

"He's in the record books for striking out the side one inning on nine straight pitches," Fisk said ruefully. "Guess who was the middle man? Me. I felt helpless. He's the hardest thrower I ever had to face. I faced him eight times in my rookie year, and he struck me out seven of them."

But then the fighter in Fisk took over.

"There are a few pitchers who will do well against me, but I'll do well against the rest," he said. "You can't let bad days discourage you. It takes a man to handle disappointments, you know."

And through it all, Carlton made one thing perfectly clear. He was a true perfectionist in the old New England tradition. He was never totally sat-

Fisk makes a gallant try, but misses a wild throw as California's Clyde Wright scores. Ball is at lower left.

isfied with his games, and he was always convinced that he could have done even better, tried harder.

"Look, the pitcher has a big advantage over the batter," he once explained. "If a pitcher's stuff is working, there's no way a man is going to hit him. A batter must wait for a pitcher's mistakes. There's the difference between a good hitter and an average hitter. The good hitter capitalizes on the mistakes; the average hitter lets a pitcher get away with one."

According to the Fisk Theory, concentration is the secret of success. "I'm a better catcher in the majors then I was in the minors," he said, "because I forced myself to concentrate harder. For the same reason, I started to hit more, and for more distance, when I got to the Red Sox. When I was a rookie I hit as many home runs as I did in two seasons as a minor leaguer. Why? Because I knew major league pitching was much better, so I had to concentrate much harder."

As a catcher, Fisk had more to say about pitchers —but this time he was talking about the Red Sox. "I have different methods for handling different pitchers," he said, "and I don't mind yelling at them. If they're not bearing down, I tell them. I know this gets most of them angry, but I care only about winning. Sometimes I try to get them so mad at me they'll try to throw the ball right through me. They can't of course. But if they throw that hard, they'll get the batters out. You show me a catcher who doesn't assert himself, and I'll show you a nothing catcher."

Other players—even some of Fisk's own teammates—called him cocky, arrogant, nasty. But his friends knew it was just his burning desire to win.

"I can't go along with the people who say baseball is only a game," Fisk argued. "If it's only a game, it shouldn't matter who wins. But it does matter. Baseball is my life, and I care very much if I win or lose."

The Red Sox were just as eager as Fisk to win, but for many years, they were a team of talented losers. Year after year they had the pennant seemingly wrapped up, only to fold in the stretch or lose crucial games.

Inconsistency became part of the Red Sox image, and the fans began calling them the "Country Club" Red Sox or, because there were so many high-salaried stars, the "Gold Sox."

But that didn't sit well with Carlton Fisk. He was determined to change that reputation. "Even in my rookie year I hated to hear things like that," said Fisk. "Terms like 'Country Club' and 'Gold Sox' just infuriated me. With the right kind of attitude, the only thing any team of mine will ever be called is Winner. And put that in capital letters, because it's what really counts."

BOBBY BONDS

On July 23, 1973, the day before he was to manage the National League All-Star team, Sparky Anderson was asked to outline his plans.

"I am going to get Bobby Bonds into the game as soon as possible," Anderson said. "At this point Bobby is the best player in baseball. He's having the best season of everyone, and I haven't yet found anything he can't do well."

The next night Bobby Bonds of the San Francisco Giants joined the All-Star game in the fourth inning. One inning later he smacked a two-run homer off Bill Singer of the California Angels. In the seventh inning, the speedy outfielder stretched an apparent single into an easy double. He drove in two runs,

scored one and lived up to Anderson's expectations by being named the game's Most Valuable Player. All in all, it was a typical Bonds performance.

Looking back, it seemed surprising that Bonds was not a starter in the All-Star contest. But the fans, who vote for the All-Star line-up, had a difficult choice for the outfield positions. Ahead of Bonds they placed two great veterans, Pete Rose of Cincinnati and Billy Williams of Chicago; and young Cesar Cedeno of the Houston Astros.

Bobby was neither surprised nor disturbed to place fourth against this competition. "How can I say I'm better than those other guys?" he wondered. "They're great players. And besides, it wasn't just anybody's choice. I mean, the fans voted. I'm just happy to be here."

If the players had been the ones to cast ballots, however, Bobby might well have been in the outfield for the first inning.

Davey Johnson, who spent seven years in the American League with Baltimore before being traded to Atlanta in 1973, was the National League second-baseman. According to Johnson, "There is no player in the American League even close to Bobby in ability. I don't think I ever saw anyone in the American League that good, except for Mickey Mantle."

Carlton Fisk, the young catching star of the Boston Red Sox, was another All-Star. He was

Bobby Bonds, a double threat as a hitter and base-runner, slides into third base as the ball gets away from Chicago's Ron Santo.

equally impressed with Bonds. "I saw that homer of his in the fifth and it made a believer out of me," said Fisk. "He hit one of Singer's best pitches.

"And that double in the seventh . . . I didn't see it, because I was in the clubhouse, but I heard the guy say on the radio that it looked like a single. Then he started yelling that Bobby was going to try for two. Then he kept saying it looked like he wasn't even going to have to slide in. That's speed."

All-Star Sal Bando of the Oakland A's was still another Bonds booster. "He's the most dynamic hitter I've seen," said Bando. "You just can't find a weak spot to pitch him. He hits to all fields with power and he has a quick bat and he can beat out grounders for hits. I'd say he's the best all-around player in their league—maybe in the majors."

Bobby Lee Bonds was born on March 15, 1946, in Riverside, California. There were three boys and a girl in the Bonds family, and it was the girl who first attracted notice in sports. Bobby's sister Rosie, who was almost two years older, set track records in both dash and hurdle events. And even Bobby couldn't beat her in 50-yard dashes.

Bobby's father was a building contractor, and by the time Bobby was eight years old, he and his sister were going along on their father's jobs. Bobby cleaned out houses and did other odd jobs, getting paid a dollar an hour. Later he packed groceries and stocked shelves in a market and worked as a plasterer in his father's company.

"I enjoyed my childhood," he said. "I liked growing up in my family. We had fun, but we had to learn the value of things, too. We all worked early, and even a dollar an hour seemed like good money."

Bobby began playing Little League baseball when he was in the second grade. By the time he was in ninth grade, he stood 6-foot-1 and weighed 160 pounds. He was discovering that his talents in baseball extended into other sports as well. He was a four-sport star (baseball, football, basketball and track) at Riverside's Polytechnic High School, and in 1964 he was named Southern California's "Schoolboy Athlete of the Year." On the track team he once ran the 100-yard dash in 9.5 seconds, showing rare speed for a man so big. And in baseball he pitched and played the outfield, hitting .407 one year.

Bobby had no doubts about his plans for the future. "Right from the start I wanted to marry Patricia and play baseball," he said. Patricia Howard had been the Bonds' next-door neighbor, and they were married while still in high school.

As for baseball, Bobby later said, "I always wanted to do it, and I always pictured myself doing what I do now. In so many ways I have been a very lucky man."

Bobby's high school baseball had attracted the attention of several major league scouts. The Giants signed him without a bonus because he had had a poor senior year, but scout Evan Pusich knew Bobby had all the natural tools to be a major leaguer. "He could hit with power and he had that great speed and he was smart," Pusich recalled. "He knew baseball . . . he knew how to run the bases . . . and he knew what he had to do to make the majors. He was willing to work hard for what he wanted."

Bobby's first organized team was a Class D farm club in Lexington, North Carolina. In 1965, his first-ever season, the 19-year-old Bonds hit .323. His 135 hits included 25 homers and 11 triples. He had 86 RBI's and led the league in runs scored with 103. To top it all off, he stole 33 bases—in 35 tries. That performance earned him an award as the league's "Most Outstanding Prospect."

Obviously, Bonds was too good for the Class D league. So in 1966 the Giants sent him to Fresno of the California League. Again, he responded with power. Although his average dropped to .262, he collected an impressive 26 homers, 91 RBI's and 119 hits. This time he "only" picked up 18 stolen bases—but there was a good reason for that lapse.

"The man hitting behind me complained that I was forcing him to swing at too many bad pitches trying to protect me when I tried to steal," Bonds explained. "So I stopped running."

In 1967 Bobby played for Waterbury, Connecticut, in the AA Eastern League. The better competition didn't bother Bonds at all, and he enjoyed another superb season. This time he rapped out 15 homers, drove in 68 runs and batted .261.

Convinced that Bonds was a big league prospect, the Giants decided to give him one more year of minor league seasoning. So in 1968, Bobby moved up to Phoenix of the AAA International League.

Rat-a-tat-tat. The hits sprayed off his bat like bullets from a machine gun. In Phoenix, Bobby batted .370, collecting 81 hits in 219 at-bats. He also picked up 47 RBI's and eight home runs in 60 games. That was all the Giants had to see. Bobby Bonds was called up to San Francisco.

On June 24, Phoenix manager Rosy Ryan gave Bobby the news. "He said I'd probably play for the Giants the next night," Bonds recalled. "I couldn't believe it. But he made me leave, so I figured it was true enough."

On June 25, Bonds found himself in Candlestick Park facing the rival Los Angeles Dodgers. In the seventh inning, with the bases loaded, Bonds came up and Dodger pitcher John Purdin relaxed a bit. Instead of somebody dangerous, like Willie Mays or Willie McCovey, all he had to do was get a nervous rookie out, Purdin thought.

But then Bonds hit a high fastball out of the park, becoming only the second man in 70 years to hit a grand-slam home run in his first major league game.

"I didn't realize it was so special," Bobby said later. "I had hit three of them in Phoenix."

Bonds finished out that half-season with the Giants in good standing, hitting 9 homers and driving in 35 runs to go with his .254 batting average.

In 1969, Bobby's first full major league season, he

Bonds comes up with a long fly ball near the warning track.

first began to bloom as an all-around threat. He started running the bases with a style and an excitement that hadn't been seen since Willie Mays was in his prime. At one point Bonds stole 13 bases in a row—four times beating a throw from the catcher on a pitch-out call.

He finished that season with 32 homers and 45 stolen bases, becoming the fourth man in baseball history to join the "30–30" club in one season. Mays and Hank Aaron were two of the others.

"I had no idea it was coming, and I had no idea so few people had done it," Bobby said of that feat. "I wish nobody had told me. I found out when I had twenty-nine homers, and I started to press."

Bobby's statistics would have been a fine achievement for any ballplayer, but for a newcomer to the majors they were really outstanding. There was one statistic, however, that Bonds would have preferred to forget.

That same season, the super-slugger set a major league record for strikeouts, breaking a 16-year-old mark set by Dave Nicholson of the Chicago White Sox. (Bonds broke his own record in 1970, when he fanned 189 times.)

"I can't explain my strikeouts," he said, "and I don't think I can stop them. I get into the habit of trying to pull everything, and that's when I strike out. If I concentrate on hitting the ball where it's pitched, I don't have the problem. Also, I guess at

This time Cincinnati catcher Johnny Bench won't catch the ball. San Francisco slugger Bobby Bonds got to it first.

pitchers, and when I do I strike out more often. But everybody gives me advice, and that can just confuse you. I'm going to get my strikeouts. It can't be helped."

Despite those big strikeouts, Bobby had another great season in 1970. He hit 26 homers, drove in 78 runs and participated in more double plays than any outfielder in the National League. And for the first time in his major league career, Bonds batted over .300 (.302 to be exact). He also joined the exclusive 200-hit club, getting exactly that number in 663 times at bat. With those figures, Bobby established himself as a true star of the Giants—and a superstar of the future.

"Bobby Bonds," said his teammate Willie Mc-Covey, "can hit a ball as far as any man I've ever seen, but still I don't look at him as a home run hitter. He can do so many other things."

The fans obviously shared McCovey's high opinion of Bonds. In 1971, Bobby made his first appearance in an All-Star game. By the end of the season he had collected 33 home runs and 102 RBI's. Bobby was just as successful in the outfield. He was awarded the league's Golden Glove for his .994 fielding average, making only two errors in well over 300 chances. With the help of their young star, the Giants won their Western Division championship, but they were defeated by Pittsburgh in the playoffs.

In 1972, Bobby slumped a little. He hit only 26 home runs and batted only .259. Yet he stole 44 bases, bringing up a problem for manager Charlie Fox. Bonds was a power hitter, but he was also a great leadoff man, getting on base often and posing a threat on the basepaths.

In 1973, Fox put his star in the leadoff spot, and Bobby responded with the best season of his career. His average climbed to .283, he drove in 96 runs and he almost became the first man in history to hit 40 home runs and steal 40 bases in the same season. He had joined the "30-30" club in his first full season—now with 43 stolen bases and 39 four baggers in '73, Bobby Bonds had just missed establishing a new "40-40" club.

Bobby felt that he still had to overcome his tendency to press too hard when the team "absolutely has to have a big hit."

"I try to win all by myself," he said, "and that's stupid. I can't relax, and even when I try to 'take' a pitch I swing at it."

But he gave most of his problems to opposing pitchers. One pitcher went so far as to hope that if Bobby got a hit it would be a home run. "I hope he doesn't get a hit that leaves him on base," he said. "When he's on first or second he drives me absolutely crazy. He ruins my concentration to the point that I might wind up three or four runs down instead of just the one his homer would mean. I'm telling you, he's just too much."

A rare compliment? Not really, considering the rare talent that belongs to Bobby Bonds.

FERGUSON JENKINS

In the early 1960s Ferguson Jenkins hardly seemed the pitcher destined most likely to succeed. In fact, there was some question as to whether he even belonged in the major leagues.

"People told me I couldn't make it as a major league starter," he said. "My manager in Puerto Rico one winter was Cal McLish, a former major league pitcher himself, and he told me to start thinking about becoming a relief specialist if I wanted to stick in the majors. Who was I to say no?"

So Fergie became a relief man, and a good one. Late in the 1965 season he joined the Phillies and was impressive in a dozen innings of relief work, picking up a 2–1 record and a 2.25 earned run average.

"The Phillies told me I would be their number one man in the bull pen in 1966," he said. "So I went home to Canada happy. Then, that winter, I read that they had traded for Darold Knowles, a top relief pitcher."

It wasn't hard for Jenkins to figure out what that meant. With the veteran Knowles on the staff, Fergie would have to be content with the number two spot in the Philly bull pen.

"I was disappointed," Jenkins admitted. "But I tried to accept it, to understand it. After all, I had just been a rookie, so how could the Phillies know if I could stand up over a full season?"

But shortly after the start of the '66 season, Jenkins found himself off the roster altogether. On April 21, he was sent to the Chicago Cubs along with outfielder Adolfo Phillips and first baseman John Herrnstein for pitchers Larry Jackson and Bob Buhl.

Chicago general manager John Holland explained the trade this way: "We knew the Phils wanted pitching help from veteran pitchers, and we wanted some of their young talent. We offered them Buhl and Jackson, and they wanted them both. We asked for the three kids."

Most people thought the man the Cubs really wanted was Phillips. "We did want him, of course," Holland said, "but we wanted Fergie just as badly. We had followed his minor league career and we

Fergie Jenkins, in one of his early starts for the Cubs, fires the ball. He won 20 games in his first season.

saw potential in him. I know some of our people thought he'd be better as a starter."

So the 6-foot-5, 210-pound right-hander became a starter again. And that trade turned out to be the turning point in the career of Ferguson Jenkins. But at the time, he viewed it as a low point, perhaps a sign that he would never achieve stardom. By this time he didn't even care if he started or pitched in relief. "I was tired of almost making it. I wanted to stick," he said.

Jenkins did more than just stick with the Cubs— he became their number one pitcher. In his first full season as a starter he racked up 20 victories. Fergie repeated—or bettered—that achievement five more times in the next five years.

In 1974, Fergie began a new career in the American League after being traded to the Texas Rangers. There was no doubt about it—Ferguson Jenkins was truly a big-league star. It had been a long climb for the tall strikeout artist, but he had learned all about courage and determination when he was still a boy.

Ferguson Arthur Jenkins was born December 13, 1943, in Chatham, Ontario, Canada. His mother, Dolores Jackson Jenkins, was blind. To Fergie she was "the most courageous person I've ever known."

His dad, Ferguson, Sr., was a struggler, too. He had played semi-pro baseball for a number of Negro League teams, including the Chatham (Ontario)

All-Stars and the Chatham Panthers. He played ball for $35 a week and did some prize fighting to increase his earnings.

Life was never easy for the Jenkins family, but Ferguson enjoyed his childhood. "I am glad I grew up in Canada," he said. "It was a great place for a boy to be, and especially for a black. I didn't even know about racial issues until I started to play minor league baseball in America."

In Canada, the national sport is hockey. Most boys there can skate before they are old enough for school. Most—but not all. Jenkins didn't learn to skate until he was nine years old, but hockey came naturally to him, and he steadily advanced through the junior divisions of schoolboy hockey leagues.

"I went up to the Junior B class," he recalled, "which is the second-highest amateur hockey in Canada. My team was affiliated with the Montreal Canadiens, and many of my friends went on to play in the National Hockey League. I don't think I would have been successful in hockey. Oh, I might have made it to the NHL, but I wouldn't have become a star."

In addition to hockey, Fergie also excelled in basketball and baseball. He enjoyed basketball and later toured Canada with the Harlem Globetrotters.

But it was baseball, of course, that turned out to be *the* sport for Ferguson Jenkins. Because of his size Jenkins was originally an outfielder and then a first baseman.

"I was a good hitter, and in fact I was scouted by the Phillies because of my hitting. It was only because of an accident that I became a pitcher at all. One of our pitchers on the Chatham Junior All-Stars hurt his arm, and the coach didn't want to risk tiring the other pitcher. So I volunteered to pitch. I knew I could throw the ball hard, at any rate."

Jenkins won that first game in a big way, going seven innings, allowing only two hits and striking out fifteen. From then on, he was a member of the pitching staff, although he still filled in at first base.

In 1962, Tony Lucadello, a Phillies' scout, was sent to Canada to sign Jenkins as a hurler. Jenkins stalled him for a while, wanting to be sure that he had a future in pitching. Seven other major league teams were interested in the young Canadian. Two of them, Boston and Pittsburgh, wanted Fergie as an outfielder-first baseman. Jenkins finally decided to stick with pitching and accepted the Phillies' offer.

Even after he made that decision, Fergie still had some doubts. He was an only child who had never been away from home before. Now he was going to a new country, and he was a little nervous.

"My mother used to tell me never start anything I don't think I can finish," he recalled, "and when I started acting a little unsure, she told me to make up my mind before I left because she didn't want me walking out on anybody. She made me think things through before I acted."

Fergie thought seriously about his future and then decided baseball was what he really wanted. So he left home and joined the Phillies' minor league team in Miami in the Florida State League.

By mid-season he had a 7–2 record, 69 strikeouts and an 0.97 ERA. Then the Phillies jumped him all the way up to the Triple-A Buffalo team of the International League.

In 1963 he pitched for Arkansas of the International League, but his inexperience finally caught up to him and the Phillies sent him back to Miami for the '64 season. There he learned to pitch—"not just to throw"—and his 12–5 record and 135 strikeouts in 140 innings proved he had learned his lessons well.

Jenkins spent all of 1965 with Arkansas, establishing an 8–6 mark, 112 strikeouts and a 2.95 ERA. When the minor league season ended he was brought up to Philadelphia for his first major league appearances. He pitched twelve innings in relief and got credit for two wins and one loss.

Then came 1966, and the unexpected Phillies' trade that sent Fergie to the Cubs.

When Jenkins arrived in Chicago, he met a man who was to put his career back on the right road—manager Leo Durocher.

"I asked Ferguson what he wanted to do on the team," Durocher said, "and he told me he wanted to be a relief pitcher. I was surprised because most young pitchers want to start, but I wasn't going to change him immediately. So I kept him in the bull pen."

Fergie's first appearance as a Cub was remarkable. He pitched five and a third innings, allowing no runs, and drove in the only two Cub runs with a homer and an RBI single. The Cubs won 2–0.

By July, Durocher saw so much promise in Fergie's fastball and poise that he decided to take him out of the bull pen and make him a starter. On July 27 he told Jenkins he would start in three days. On July 30, against the New York Mets, Fergie started for the first time.

It was a good performance. While Jenkins didn't win the game, he pitched eight innings and left with the score tied at 3–3.

"We have another starter now," Leo said after that game, "and he may become the best of them all."

Ferguson had 51 relief appearances as a Cub and nine starts, six of which were wins. He finished the '66 season with a low 2.25 ERA.

Then, in 1967, Jenkins started his incredible run of 20-win seasons. Even Fergie couldn't quite explain his dramatic progress. "I know one thing that had a lot to do with it was Leo," he said. "He showed confidence in me. He became my friend. He worked with me and made me think like a winner."

In the '67 spring training session Fergie met

Jenkins keeps his eye on the target as he winds up to throw.

another man who proved to be of great help—a new pitching coach named Joe Becker.

Becker had worked the previous season with the St. Louis Cardinals and had seen Fergie's transformation from a relief man to a starter. "He was just brimming over with natural talent," Joe said. "I couldn't wait to start working with him."

Jenkins credits Becker with giving him invaluable help. "When I met him, he told me he'd make me a million dollars if I did four things. They were work hard, concentrate every minute, make the batter hit the pitch I wanted him to hit and be ready to go all out every fourth day.

"Technically, he made me cut down my big windup and showed me how to mask my pitches. He and I would study movies of my games."

Becker also got Fergie to bear down. "I don't like to admit it," Jenkins said, "but sometimes I just get lazy. I used to relax. Joe would yell at me, and it would jolt me back."

After a super spring training Jenkins was the Cubs' Opening Day pitcher in 1967. He won that game, against his old Philly teammates, giving up just five hits. He went on to a 20–13 record and a 2.80 ERA. His 236 strikeouts in 289 innings broke the team strikeout record of 205, set way back in 1909. On September 29, he got his 20th win to clinch third place for the Cubs. It was the Cubs' highest finish in 20 years.

The 1968 season didn't start well for Jenkins—in fact it almost didn't start at all. During spring training Fergie was thrown from a horse while riding in Scottsdale, Arizona. He hurt his back, his leg *and* his pitching arm. But, fortunately, the injuries weren't as serious as they might have been, and he was released from the hospital in a day. Nevertheless, both Durocher and Holland exploded at him for being foolish enough to jeopardize his career.

Jenkins was in a lot of pain for a while and missed his Opening Day assignment. But he came back to earn a 20–15 record and a 2.63 ERA. This time he had 260 strikeouts. He started 40 games and worked 308 innings, both Cub records.

Chicago, meanwhile, had changed from a weak-hitting, second-division club to a challenger. Jenkins was one of the major causes of this transformation, and his strong pitching supported the dangerous bats of Ernie Banks, Ron Santo and Billy Williams.

In the middle of August, however, the Cubs lost a crucial series to St. Louis and fell out of contention. Still, it had been a good season, and the confident Cubs looked forward to the next year.

In 1969, Fergie started 43 games, worked 311 innings and wound up with a 21–15 record and a 3.21 ERA. He also led the league in strikeouts with 273. But once again the Cubs collapsed late in the season, losing a crucial four-game series to Pittsburgh in early September. That cut their Eastern

Division lead over the New York Mets to just
two-and-a-half games.

Coming up was a two-game road trip to New
York. The Mets won the first game, cutting the
Chicago lead by a full game. Then the New Yorkers
won the second game, too. The next day the Mets
won a game in Montreal while the Cubs lost their
seventh straight in Philadelphia.

The Cubs had fallen out of first place, and they
never got back. The Mets won the National League
pennant and went on to stun the Baltimore Orioles
in a five-game World Series.

Fergie had lost three starts in a row in September,
and his disappointment took some of the glow off
another outstanding achievement—his third straight
20-plus season.

In 1970, Fergie led the league in complete games
(24), again led the Cub pitchers in everything—innings (313), strikeouts (274) and victories (22 against
16 losses).

Again the Cubs found themselves in a pennant
race. On September 13, they were just one game
behind the league-leading Pittsburgh Pirates. The
Cubs had come too close to too many pennants to
give up on this one. Tension mounted on the
Chicago team.

But Jenkins had something even more important
to worry about at that moment. His mother was
dying. He rushed home to be with her, and got there

just in time. Mrs. Jenkins died September 15.

Fergie stayed home for the funeral and then rejoined the Cubs for their pennant run. "I didn't want to," he said. "I didn't feel like pitching, but I remembered what she had told me, about doing my best and not starting anything if I couldn't finish it. So I went back."

He pitched his first night back, and Chicago beat Montreal, 3–2, while Jenkins picked up his 20th victory of the season. But the next day, after leading 4–1, the Cubs lost, 6–4. It was the beginning of another skid. Fergie won his 22nd game on the last day of the season, but the Cubs only finished second.

Although he won so many games, some fans accused Fergie of losing important ones in the clutch. Jenkins refused to take all the blame, reminding his critics that he couldn't win games without some help from his teammates. "How many people remembered that I tied a major league record for losing five 1–0 games in 1968?" he wondered. "It seems like I always lose a lot of one-run games. I don't like it any more than they do."

Yet he continued to win—and lose—while the Cubs continued their unsuccessful pennant attempts.

In 1971, Fergie had his best major league season. He received a $92,500 contract in the spring, and then proved he was worth every dollar by putting together a 24–13 record and a 2.77 ERA. Working

325 innings, he struck out 263 batters.

He led the league in innings and wins, as well as in complete games (30). He was the starting pitcher for the National League's All-Star team and pitched three innings, fanning six men and allowing no runs.

For all of that, as well as for the reputation he had already established, Jenkins won the 1971 Cy Young Memorial Award, surprising many people by beating out Met ace Tom Seaver for the honor. (Tom had a 20–10 record and led the league with a 1.76 ERA and 289 strikeouts.)

"Winning the Cy Young Award was one of the happiest moments of my life," Jenkins said. "It was November when I heard about it, and I knew it was a tribute I couldn't match anywhere else. I just wish my mother had been around to share in the joy I felt."

There were other goals in Jenkins' dreams, many of them no different from those of all major league players. He wanted to take part in a World Series. He wanted to know he was part of the best team in the major leagues. He wanted to continue winning, and he wanted to cut down on his losses.

Jenkins also had some more ambitious dreams. "I would like to be elected to the Hall of Fame," he declared after the 1972 season, which brought him yet another 20-game performance (20–12 this time) and a contract for more than $100,000.

"I think that is the greatest recognition a player

Frustrated with the Cub management in 1973, Jenkins throws a bat onto the field after being taken out of a game.

can ever earn. But just to be in the majors is an honor few men know. I would like to pitch as long as I can win, and after that I would like to stay in the game, maybe as a manager. I don't think a black manager would face any special problems, and I think there are many black men now who would make fine managers—like Ernie Banks, Frank Robinson, Maury Wills and Bill White, to name a few."

Fergie's dream of the Hall of Fame seemed to dim in 1973 when he slumped badly, winding up with a 14–16 record, 170 strikeouts and a too-high 3.89 ERA. Yet he said that the major cause of his tailspin was his unhappiness in Chicago, and when he was traded to the American League's Texas Rangers his natural confidence returned.

A setback, perhaps. But hardly the end of the line. For as he proved by making it to the majors, Ferguson Jenkins was always a man who knew how to make his dreams come true.

INDEX

Page numbers in italics refer to photographs.

148